DEAD COACH WALKING

TOM PENDERS SURVIVING AND THRIVING IN COLLEGE HOOPS

TOM PENDERS
STEVE RICHARDSON

REEDY PRESS
St. Louis, Missouri

Reedy Press
PO Box 5131
St. Louis, MO 63139, USA

Library of Congress Control Number: 2011921292

ISBN: 978-1-935806-02-8

Please visit our website at www.reedypress.com.

Cover design by Jill Halpin

Printed in the United States of America
11 12 13 14 15   5 4 3 2 1

CONTENTS

To Dr. James T. Willerson,

who saved my life and allowed me to continue coaching college basketball. Dr. Willerson is the president of the Texas Heart Institute and is one of the most respected heart specialists in the world. We have become lifelong friends. Every person needs to have a motivator in life, and Dr. Willerson is that person for me. I was indeed blessed to have had the opportunity to continue coaching beyond my ten years at Texas because of him and the Texas Heart Institute.

ACKNOWLEDGMENTS

I would love to be able to list all of the people who have had a positive influence on my life and my coaching career, but I'm sure that I would unintentionally omit some important people. I would like to thank my co-author, Steve Richardson, for all of his research and work on this project.

I was fortunate to have been born into a close, loving, and caring family. My father, Jim, was the best role model that a son could possibly have, both as a father and as a revered coach. My mother, Lillian, taught me to aim high and never rest on my laurels. My siblings—Jimmy, Billy, and Kathy—were, and always will be, extremely close to me. Special thanks go out to Fred Shabel, my UConn basketball coach. He has no idea how much he motivated me to excel as a player and later as a coach. There is no greater way to flatter a person than to follow in his footsteps, and that is exactly what I did.

Lastly, a special acknowledgment must be made to my wife, Susie, and my children, Tommy and Karli. Susie has teamed with me for more than thirty years. She is my partner, best friend, and one strong and resilient woman. Tommy, who is an outstanding high school basketball coach, has always been the ultimate son, a wonderful father to my grandchildren, and a special friend. Karli is the most compassionate and loving daughter a father can have. I am so proud of them. Only your wife and children know what a treacherous minefield the world of college basketball coaching actually is. They lived it with me, hence I was never alone for a single day.

—Tom Penders, November 2010

PREFACE

I first became acquainted with Tom Penders in late March 1988. I was working for the *Dallas Morning News* and covering the search for a new men's basketball coach at the University of Texas. We were all in Kansas City, Missouri, during the Final Four.

Kansas State coach Lon Kruger had just decided to stay in Manhattan for some inexplicable reason after he flew to Austin for a job interview and returned to the Flint Hills. And the re-focus was on Purdue coach Gene Keady, who had gone to school at Kansas State and had been a classmate of Texas athletic director DeLoss Dodds.

In those days, Dodds was not nearly so well entrenched in Austin. He needed a good hire because the previous basketball coach, Bob Weltlich, had not been a good fit at Texas, and football was basically just holding its own under David McWilliams, who later would be fired.

Before hiring Weltlich, a former Bob Knight assistant who had taken Ole Miss to the NCAA Tournament, Dodds fired the home-spun Abe Lemons shortly after becoming the Longhorns athletic director. Whether you agreed with that firing or not, Lemons had been popular in Austin. Weltlich really never was, and he mostly struggled in six seasons at Texas. Home basketball attendance at the Erwin Center tumbled to about 4,000 a game. So this hire was critical not only for the future success of Texas basketball, but also to some degree for Dodds' credibility as an athletic director.

Wandering around the Hyatt Regency Hotel in Kansas City just trying to find a lead for the UT coaching story, I bumped into the Cotton Bowl executive director Jim "Hoss" Brock, who was heading up an escalator. To say that Hoss was plugged into the state of

Texas in those days was an understatement. "Heard anything, Hoss?" I asked hopefully. Brock got one of those looks you knew something was up. I was onto something. I tried to push the Keady angle, but he would have none of that. He uttered, "Tom Penders . . . That's who they are talking to. You better get on that. He's the coach at Rhode Island."

So the chase began for Tom Penders. I don't know that I had it first. But let's put it this way—no one had it before I did. A few days later, Penders became the head coach at Texas, took the team to eight NCAA Tournaments in ten years, and put basketball on the map in Austin, where previously it had been an afterthought.

I remember during Weltlich's final season how so much of the television pre-game advertisements and coverage seemed to center around the women's basketball team at Texas. Men's basketball got the attention of a summer shed leaf. Penders really had his work cut out for him in Austin. I remember thinking it was going to be interesting to see how it all I played out.

As I got to know Tom I realized he could promote his team better than anybody I had ever seen. Penders didn't participate in press conferences, he directed then like he had a baton in his hand. While some coaches wanted to end chats with the media before they began, Penders would stay overtime to explain his strategy. He was a quote machine and not afraid to speak his mind.

 Penders was such a 180-degree turn from the conservative Weltlich that he had no problems winning over the fans and turning the program around. His style would rankle game officials in the SWC, who were used to slower, more methodical approaches. Penders' players were getting up and down the court so fast, some of the out-of-shape, burly SWC officials were gasping for breath. I thought the SWC was going to have to post oxygen tanks by the scorer's bench for some of these guys—especially when an Arkansas under Nolan Richardson and Texas played.

While Weltlich came from a traditional halfcourt set, typically found in Big 10 and Midwest offenses, Penders was running, shooting threes, and making the 45-second clock look like it belonged in a turtle race. The ninety-four-foot game was on in Austin. This was shortly after the 45-second shot clock and the three-point shot had been introduced to men's college basketball.

Penders' style had been to quickly adapt to these rule changes, where some older, more set-in-their-ways coaches had been resistant to the changes. This showed itself in Penders' two years of success in Rhode Island and especially at Texas.

Guard play became much more important because of the shorter distance of the three-point shot and the fact teams needed to find ways to work the ball quicker on offense to get shots because of the shot clock. No longer could a team hold the ball for a long, long period of time and then lob it into a big man for a basket. Getting the ball up and down the court for transition baskets by guards and open three-pointers became a premium in recruiting as well.

During Penders' first year at Texas, he basically took the team Weltlich coached, added the two players sitting out, transfer guards Lance Blanks (Virginia) and Joey Wright (Drake), and away they went. It wasn't always easy, but they adapted to his style. Guard Travis Mays went from thinking about transferring to becoming a star and flourishing with the more wide-open approach. Players went from looking over their shoulder to the bench at Weltlich after they missed a shot to relaxing and letting the game come to them.

Penders' first team at Texas won twenty-five games, up nine victories from the previous season. His 1988–89 team made only Texas' second NCAA Tournament trip since 1974 when Coach Leon Black's team lost in the first round after winning the SWC with a losing overall record. Despite Lemons' popularity, Texas only went to one NCAA Tournament in 1979 during his tenure and lost that game. With an NCAA Tournament victory in 1989 at Texas, Penders posted the Longhorns' first tournament victory since 1972.

Penders' arrival changed everything. The fortunes of men's basketball started trending straight upward. I will never forget two things from later seasons at Texas. In 1989–90, Texas and LSU played in the old Summit in Houston before scouts from most of the NBA teams. LSU had big men Shaquille O'Neal and Stanley Roberts and guard Chris Jackson. Texas had "B-M-W," as in Lance Blanks, Travis Mays, and Joey Wright. The final score was 124–113 LSU. Whew! It's still the highest point total by a UT men's basketball team on a neutral floor.

Two years later, Texas lost to LSU, 84–83, on January 3, 1992, at the Louisiana Superdome before 61,304 fans in one of the great spectacles of a college basketball regular season. That crowd, all these years later, still ranks as the fourth highest regular-season game in attendance.

Penders always brought that kind of excitement to the programs he coached, whether at Tufts, Columbia, Fordham, Rhode Island, Texas, George Washington, or Houston. In his last season at Houston, he parlayed the nation's leading scorer, guard Aubrey Coleman, into a great run in the Conference USA Tournament, which produced the Cougars' first NCAA berth since 1992.

Over the years, it always has been a pleasure to cover Tom Penders-coached teams wherever he has been.

—Steve Richardson, November 2010

INTRODUCTION

Getting his head coaching start on the high school level in Connecticut during the 1968–69 season, Tom Penders quickly proved his mettle after only three years and moved to the collegiate ranks at Tufts. During the next four decades, he began the task of turning around a series of college programs that often were considered to be on death row, hence the book's title.

Penders is one of only eight Division I coaches to have taken four different schools to the National Collegiate Athletic Association (NCAA) Division I Men's Basketball Tournament—Rhode Island, Texas, George Washington, and Houston. He is one of only five men to have made seven head coaching stops in college basketball—Tufts, Columbia, Fordham, Rhode Island, Texas, George Washington, and Houston. He is strictly alone in another category since 1948. He has coached at six different Division I schools in the modern era.

In thirty-nine years of head coaching—thirty-six on the collegiate level—Penders has developed a wealth of basketball knowledge. The intent of this book is to make that information available to coaches, players, and general college basketball fans through an examination of his head coaching career that often took uncommon twists and turns while raising programs out of low-tide situations.

In 1997, he even stared death in the face, which is described in detail in the opening chapter. Six years after he had been diagnosed with cardiomyopathy in a routine physical exam, Penders had a defibrillator implanted in his chest at the Texas Heart Institute in Houston when further tests indicated he had a great risk of cardiac arrest. Starting at age fifty-two, he coached with the device in his chest for a total of ten seasons without any major incidents at Texas, George Washington, and finally Houston. His ability to coach with the defibrillator has served as an inspiration to heart patients everywhere.

Penders' survival instincts were developed at an early age in the hardscrabble workingman's town of Statford, Connecticut. There, where his father Jim was a legendary high school baseball coach and athletic director, Penders developed the tough outer hide as a baseball-basketball star who later transferred those talents to the University of Connecticut. He eventually forewent a career in professional baseball to coach and subsequently survived turnarounds at Tufts, Columbia, Fordham, Rhode Island, Texas, and Houston.

From recruiting on the streets of New York City to high-scoring games against Arkansas and Coach Nolan Richardson, from battles with officials in the Southwest Conference to coaching some of the best players in the country, Penders talks about all his stops and how he dealt with athletic directors, conference commissioners, assistants, Amateur Athletic Union (AAU) coaches, the National Association of Basketball Coaches (NABC), and the NCAA.

The book takes people behind the scenes, where Penders describes his game strategies, other coaching personalities, locker room scenes, and the recruiting trail. His perspective, while sometimes controversial, is a readable account of a coach's life in college basketball spanning four decades.

Since 1968, when he was a Connecticut high school head coach, Penders has coached through the administrations of nine U.S. presidents, starting with Lyndon Baines Johnson. The length and breadth of his coaching résumé is impressive. He belongs to the prestigious 600-victory club (648) and has coached in 1,086 games. His games-coached total, through the end of the 2009–10 season, ranked fourth among active coaches in Division I behind only Connecticut's Jim Calhoun, Duke's Mike Krzyzewski, and Syracuse's Jim Boeheim.

Jump aboard and listen while Tom Penders takes you on a journey through a record-tying seven schools and an inspiring health recovery in *Dead Coach Walking*.

"I am one of the luckiest people in the world because I have never looked at a day of coaching as a day of actual work," Penders said recently. "I think about how lucky I've been to spend thirty-nine years as a coach and three more years as a commentator covering something that I would probably do for free. How many people can say that? I have also been in a profession where your performance can be objectively rated based on your record. It's simple; in the end you are either a success or a failure. Success is not just your won/loss record but your ability to survive. You don't last very long unless you are successful." Entering the 2010–11 season, only eleven major college coaches all-time had coached in more games than Tom Penders. He ranked No. 25 in career victories.

PART I

DEAD COACH RISING

"Yes, he is an inspiration to me. I think it could be inspirational to anyone who came to know about it."

—Dr. James T. Willerson, on Tom Penders' desire to coach with his heart condition

T om Penders lay in an Austin, Texas, hospital bed in the fall of 1997 literally not knowing if his next breath would be his last. His heart, after a chain reaction of a series of allergic events to the medication Ketoprofen, was in an incredibly weakened condition, and at least one doctor at Seton Hospital was recommending a heart transplant.

Penders—who had enjoyed a life filled with individual athletic achievements in college basketball, college and minor league baseball, and fast-pitch softball, plus a thriving, healthy, active lifestyle off the court and field—was stunned by the sudden developments he faced.

As a kid he had been diagnosed with a heart murmur. But that had never stopped him from playing baseball and basketball at the University of Connecticut, signing a minor-league contract with the Cleveland Indians, and playing for the national powerhouse Raybestos fast-pitch softball team until nearly forty years of age.

In 1990, during a routine exam for an insurance policy from the University of Texas, he had been diagnosed with cardiomyopathy. Initially, he was startled because Loyola Marymount basketball star Hank Gaithers had died suddenly of this condition shortly before Penders' 1990 diagnosis. Those fears soon subsided, however. Doctors put Penders on some medications—alpha blockers and beta blockers—and he never had a major incident nor a real problem for seven years.

This was different.

A heart transplant now? At age fifty-two? A few weeks before, he had been playing golf, lifting weights, using a treadmill, and preparing for the 1997–98 basketball season at Texas, which would be his twenty-seventh at the collegiate level. Yet only days before the 1997–98 season was to begin, officials at the hospital had already begun prepping Penders' wife, Susie, whom he married during the Final Four weekend in 1980, for the possibility of the transplant and the psychological effects it would have on the patient and the family. Was his coaching career over? All sorts of things were running through his mind when Penders decided his fate would not be decided at the Austin hospital where doctors said his heart was shutting down.

A couple of years earlier, he had met the renowned cardiologist Denton Cooley, a University of Texas graduate, during a golf outing. Dr. Cooley had said, "Tom, you ever have any questions, call me." Susie called Cooley in Houston.

Cooley had been a three-year basketball letterman (1939–41) at Texas and graduated Phi Beta Kappa in 1941 with a B.A. in zoology. He received his medical degree at Johns Hopkins Medical School in 1944. A quarter of a century later, Cooley became a pioneer in the technique of open-heart surgery. In 1968, he performed the first successful heart transplant in the United States. A year later, he implanted the first totally artificial heart in a human.

Always a fighter, Penders argued with the doctor in Austin after Cooley "ordered" him to Houston for an evaluation of his condition. "The doctor in Austin said, 'You can't get out of bed,'" Penders recalled. "I am sitting up in bed. I put my shoes on and a t-shirt, and I said, 'Follow me.' I walk down six flights of stairs outside the hospital and around it. He followed me all the way. I said, 'I am leaving.' Susie has to sign these papers releasing the Austin hospital of any responsibility. We drive to Houston."

Susie was a nervous wreck during the two-hour car ride on November 4, 1997, before Penders was admitted to St. Luke's Episcopal Hospital in Houston. "They were concerned that Tom may not make it (there)," Susie said of the Austin doctors. "I was speeding. I didn't care how fast I drove. Tom was sitting next to me and looking like he was going to die."

Penders was admitted to the Houston hospital under an assumed name—Thomas V. Brown—so the media would not find out about his sickness and speculate about his future as UT's coach. Doctors quickly set about evaluating his condition. It was determined he did not need a heart transplant, but that something was wrong with his kidneys. His heart, however, was in a seriously weakened condition because it had had to work extra hard as his kidneys were shutting down.

In October, Penders had made a trip to Florida and Maryland for some basketball clinics, and he believed he was suffering from the flu because of stomach cramping and a fever. An emergency hospital in Florida had given him the drug Ketoprofen, which would help the flu-like symptoms. Apparently, Penders suffered an allergic reaction and the drug had shut down his kidneys causing him to retain fluids. Penders went to the Austin hospital.

Dr. James T. Willerson, at the hospital in Houston and now the president of the Texas Heart Institute, saved Penders' coaching career. Willerson made the evaluation that Penders did not need a heart transplant, but was going to face a regimen that would change his diet and require maximum sleep, moderate exercise, and elimination of stress. In addition, he would need prescription medicine, vitamin supplementation, and a defibrillator. "I was very concerned whether or not he could return to coaching," Willerson said. "He was very ill when he came to see us. Originally, his heart muscle was weak. We were very concerned about that. He was out of breath and got tired quickly. We addressed that very quickly with certain medications and procedures. And he responded well."

Willerson and Cooley decided Penders needed the defibrillator, a preventative device in the event his heart needed to be shocked back into rhythm. "A defibrillator shocks the heart if it stops. I was told it feels like you are kicked by a mule if it ever goes off. But it has never gone off on me. Denton Cooley opened the door, and Dr. Willerson, head cardiologist, gave me hope," Penders said.

Although doctors assured Penders that he could coach again, they told him after the defibrillator was implanted it would be better if he didn't work for four to six weeks. "I think he continued to coach even when he was ill," Willerson said. "He is a tough guy. He's a tough guy and loves coaching young people and the school he was working for at the time. He was determined to keep doing it. I was concerned about his safety. But I came to feel better about all of that."

Penders said there was a clause in his UT coaching contract that stated if he was disabled and not able to coach he was subject to termination. "It was at a time DeLoss (Dodds, UT athletic director) and I had a little bit of a strained relationship going. I didn't want to give DeLoss any reason to terminate me. I knew I could coach."

Shortly after the operation to implant the device, Penders returned to Austin and held a press conference explaining his health status and announcing that he would return as UT's head basketball coach after the first two games. He sat out those games in the Coaches vs. Cancer IKON Classic at the Meadowlands in East Rutherford, New Jersey, when assistant Eddie Oran coached the team in losses to Georgia and Princeton.

"Dr. Willerson not only saved Tom's life, but he also allowed him to go on living life to the fullest and working in a high-stress position as a college basketball coach," Susie Penders said. "Tom is indebted to him in so many ways, for not only being his doctor, but for showing kindness and love to him over the years. If necessary, he is only a cell phone call away. That, too, was important to give Tom the security to go on."

The 1997–98 season was obviously going to be a rebuilding year because several promising freshmen—Bernard Smith, Luke Axtell, and Chris Mihm—were trying to establish themselves. Meanwhile, Penders was adjusting to the medication for his condition and to the wires in his chest.

Penders was told the defibrillator would last five years before it would need to be replaced. It actually wasn't replaced until late 2004, and he will need another one in 2011. "I was scared to death my last year at Texas," Penders said. "The first month after surgery the doctors changed all my medications because I couldn't function. If I took my pills after a big breakfast, I would want to take a nap by 1 o'clock. I couldn't stay awake. If I took the pills at 7 at night, I struggled to be up until after 9. Then they tried some other medications, saying, 'Take these in morning and you won't be sleepy.' I would have a bowl of cereal at 11 a.m. By 12, you couldn't wake me up with a sledgehammer and a fire alarm.

"As an athlete you think you will never die and that you always will be strong and competitive. Even while I was coaching, I was playing tennis and racquetball, and playing fast-pitch softball until I was nearly forty. I had to train, run, and lift. Then you think, 'I don't want to have a heart attack and die. I don't want to get kicked in the chest by a mule.' You start thinking about those things: 'Should I get up and yell at the ref? Should I chew out these kids when they need it?' My last season at Texas I chose never to raise my voice at a player."

For several months, doctors did not allow Penders to lift weights, run, or carry anything heavier than ten pounds for fear the wires might rip through his chest and dislodge the stitches where the device had been inserted.

"I was concerned every time he got excited and jumped up," Susie said. "But he was so relieved he could fight this once they told him he didn't need a heart transplant. He would do whatever he needed to do to get better. The risks with the defibrillator were a blood clot and/or wire displacement. He needed to watch his diet and sleep. He needed rest, a minimum of eight hours a night and preferably nine or ten. His meds were too strong at first that he was slurring his words. Dr. Willerson said that came with it. But it would get better as his body adjusted to the meds."

In an early season game at North Texas in 1997, the stitches in his chest where the device had been inserted burst and blood ran down his chest and into his left shoe during the game. Trainers put a butterfly bandage on it back in Austin, and Penders coached the rest of the season without incident and eventually started to regain some confidence, although the team finished with a 14–17 record in his last season at Texas. The Longhorns did finish strong, beating Texas Tech and Oklahoma State before losing to Oklahoma in the Big 12 Post-Season Tournament semifinals.

"I got pushed out, fired, whatever you want to call it," Penders said. "That certainly wasn't easy to deal with. There was a lot of stress. If the thing didn't go off after that time, it probably wouldn't. It gave me confidence after that two-or-three-week period; 'shit storm,' I called it."

Following the parting of ways with Texas, Penders' heart was still in coaching despite a lucrative offer to become a television-radio analyst.

As part of his settlement with Texas, which still owed him for four years of his contract, the Longhorns brokered a deal with Host Communications for Penders to join the media company. The total package was worth about $2.4 million (the worth of his four remaining years), $1.5 million to be a television and radio analyst over four years. But Penders elected to take just the $900,000 in a cash settlement with Texas and declined the media job as another coaching opportunity almost immediately presented itself in the spring of 1998.

Jack Kvancz, the athletic director at George Washington University who played basketball against Penders in high school and college, flew to Austin, spent several days there, and convinced Penders to take the GW head coaching job that had been vacated when Mike Jarvis left to become the St. John's coach. Despite continuing concerns over his health, Penders took the job and lasted three seasons there. He took the Colonials to an Atlantic 10 division championship and an NCAA Tournament berth in 1999.

"GW was a difficult job, especially after you had been at Texas," Susie said. "It was an urban school and was not in as big of a conference as the Big 12. The office was in a three-story, walk-up building. It was a physically challenging job. There was no elevator to the office and you had to fight the traffic in D.C. every day. They got a waiver at GW so the third assistant coach could go on the road and Tom didn't go on the road to recruit. Dr. Willerson had to give his blessing."

"Jack convinced me I could win a championship in the first year with the talent they had there," Penders said. "I was going home a little bit. Several of my former players were living in that area. And I was not far from where I grew up in Connecticut. Tommy (Penders' son) ended up being my assistant. And he couldn't have been my assistant at the University of Texas because of the nepotism laws. But after three years, the health thing was still on my mind because I hadn't regained the proper strength."

Under doctor's orders, Penders reduced his speaking engagements at GW, which had risen to about 100–120 a year at Texas.

"I was still battling a fear factor and not doing things I had done all my life," Penders said of playing tennis, lifting weights in circuit training, and walking on a treadmill at a high rate of speed. "I was afraid to do anything. Mentally, GW was a little bit of a come down in terms of budget compared to Texas. I had a great first year. After the first year, I faced a massive rebuilding job. I looked at it more like doing a favor for a friend (Kvancz). I felt obligated to do that job, but I didn't have my full strength. I loved GW and the people there, but I was afraid I would die on the job. I felt guilty and didn't want to cheat GW and Jack Kvancz."

Still, Penders believed he was much luckier than other people with a defibrillator, and he conducted a candid interview with the Discovery Channel in his Maryland home. He also went to a support group, but he found his situation was far less dire than many others in the group.

The Discovery Channel aired a segment about people living with defibrillators. "There also was a woman and an older man. But mine was the bright story of the three. The woman was a thirty-four-year-old harp player whose defibrillator went off every other month. Mine has never gone off. My message on the show was: 'Don't give up. You can survive this thing. It is not a death sentence because you have had a heart attack. I didn't. If you have a heart condition see if you are a candidate for a defibrillator-pacemaker.' I wanted to talk about this. If I had cancer, I would talk about it, to try and help someone through it," Penders said.

After leaving GW following the 2000–01 season, Penders purchased a condo on South Beach, Florida, and commuted to ESPN in Bristol, Connecticut, as a commentator during two basketball seasons from 2001 to 2003. "The years I was doing TV, I had all kinds of time to work out," Penders said. "When I resigned at George Washington they honored my contract; I bought a condo in Miami in South Beach. Susie decided to work and stay in D.C. She didn't have to. But she said half kiddingly, 'Hey if this guy is going to kick off, I have to have something to do.' She also wanted to provide our family with health insurance. That was motivation. She ended up working in commercial real estate.

"When working TV, I would go down there in January and February and stayed down there, fly up to ESPN Wednesday–Thursday–Friday one year and then the next year I was working Monday–Tuesday–Wednesday. Then I would fly back down to Miami. I had a routine down there where I would walk three miles on the beach every day. I worked out in a gym. I was in great shape."

He was ready to coach again, but under different circumstances.

"My cardiologists told me back in 1997 that if I was going to coach I needed to delegate things to my assistants, get nine-ten hours of sleep, and eat right, or I would never see age sixty or see my grandchildren," Penders said. "In 1997 my cardiologist strapped me with a Holter monitor that measures heart rates and stress levels while doing everything from reading a newspaper to driving a car and sitting in your office doing normal day-to-day stuff. Then I wore the device while engaged in coaching activities—practices and even on game day before, during, and after games. I wore this device three or four different times over a two-year period. The monitor detected the most dangerous and stressful times occurred for me when I was trapped in my office, making phone calls, or having to meet with department bureaucrats.

"Practice was a day at the beach and so were the games. But my mind and body could not deal with the mundane stuff that involved being cooped up in a small office, unless I could be assured that nobody would interrupt me while breaking down a film. I loved to talk to my players but not in my office. I loved to sit and talk with them in the gym before or after practice. All of this was picked up while wearing this Holter monitor. During games my heart rate would go up a little but it wasn't even close to the crazy reaction it had when I was trapped in my office.

"Problem after problem comes through your office every day. 'You need to delegate that kind of stuff,' my doctors said, 'unless some major thing comes up. Delegate to assistants and limit time in office.' I should have been delegating all along."

Returning to coaching at Houston in 2004, Penders watched his diet daily, bringing fruits to work. He would spend most of his film-watching time during the mornings in his central Houston town home before going to practice. Then he would go home, eat dinner, and do more planning and tape watching. The Penders opted for healthier meals at home, rarely going out to dinner.

Today, Penders works out with circuit training lightweights and walks on a treadmill for three miles, forty-five minutes at a time. He has always had a health club membership somewhere since he was coach at George Washington. "Coaching is demanding, both physically and mentally," Penders said. "I was a lot more dedicated in Houston with my workouts. I have a treadmill at home and the stairmaster, plus I belong to a health club; I was able to maintain good strength and stamina. And my cardiologists are right down the street at the renowned Texas Heart Institute."

Susie Penders' current cupboard at their tastefully decorated Italian-villa-styled, three-story house in midtown Houston is noboby's fat farm. She's a nutritionist's dream and the perfect partner for Tom Penders, who must watch his diet. She makes daily trips to Whole Foods Market in Houston. Open up the pantry door: let's see flax, bran, organic soups and broths, organic bread crumbs and brown rice pasta, medicinal teas, and Truvia (a calorie-free sweetener).

Susie's refrigerator looks like a farmers' market, with all the vegetables, fruits, nuts, nutrient supplements and vitamins, not to mention the organic foods. Those interested in real hamburger and processed cheese need not enter Susie's fridge. But if you want a healthy meal or snack—by all means. A late-night snack for Tom Penders might be a wrap: turkey, spinach, and imitation cheddar-flavored mozzarella soy-free rice shreds served in a low-sodium, no-cholesterol tortilla. Alfalfa sprouts are on the side.

"He was told to really watch his salt because of congestive heart failure," Susie said. "He had to get his weight down. And he lost twenty pounds. He still likes fried clams. And we will still eat that on rare occasions."

Along with his lifestyle, Penders also changed his demeanor on the bench. "Except for Bob Knight and a few others, most coaches have a calmer sideline presence as they get older," Penders said. "Look at Jim Boeheim and Jim Calhoun now; they are not half as animated as they used to be. Rick Pitino is nowhere near as verbal and demonstrative as he was fifteen years ago. It is not even close. Watch an old game and now."

Penders conversed with several other coaches with heart problems, some with defibrillators—Georgia Tech's Paul Hewitt, West Virginia's Bob Huggins, Miami (Ohio)'s Charlie Coles, and St. Louis's Rick Majerus.

"Hewitt called me after I passed out in Alabama. . . . I was dehydrated," Penders said of a fainting episode at UAB while coach at Houston. "Paul Hewitt called me because he is a friend and he was concerned. He, too, has a defibrillator, but like me has had no incidents. He is a great young coach and can live to be one hundred. He always looks trim and under control. We can't change our genetics, but we can help ourselves by living right."

"Rick Majerus has had seven or eight bypasses. He called me and offered for me to come out there to Utah when he was the coach there. I told him I had the best doctors in the world here in Houston. Majerus is a super friend."

But maybe the most meaningful talk was in Orlando with Wake Forest coach Skip Prosser, a couple days before he passed away in July 2007. "He was talking to me about how tired he was," Penders said. "He talked about the camps. I said, 'Skip, you are going to drive yourself into the ground. Don't kill yourself.' Skip Prosser died because he tried to be everywhere for everybody. He dropped dead during summer evaluations despite having a private plane at his disposal. He told me how much he hated living in his office. He told me that he was finally going to delegate at least one half of his work to his top assistant Dino Gaudio and focus more on communicating with his players and make his work fun again, the way it was for him when he was coach at Xavier.

"Two days later, he died of a heart attack in his office. That incident changed me forever. I was going to spend whatever years I had left in coaching trying to have fun and getting to really enjoy my players. Of course, I knew that I would love them even more and develop a lifetime bond with them if we could cut down the nets one more time. I wanted to go out a winner. I was almost obsessed with this thought."

Dr. James Willerson has admired Penders' drive these last few years. "I have had some experiences with some other coaches in this situation, but I think it is very unusual for someone who has had the problems he has had medically," Willerson said. "Many people will quit and say, 'I can't do this; it is not safe to do it.' He showed his determination and courage as well as his desire not to change. It was inspirational, unusual, almost unique, and very special."

POINT GUARD FOR LIFE

"He knew what he wanted his guards to do. He featured his style with point guard play. He was intense and a good teacher. He taught me some things that were a little more cerebral at the time. He talked about the clock and the right guys to get the ball to at the right time. He gave me the fundamentals to play the game mentally as a point guard."

—Alton Byrd, Columbia University guard on Coach Tom Penders

Tom Penders grew up a coach's son in the industrial town of Stratford, Connecticut. His father Jim was a highly successful high school baseball coach and athletic director. Sports were the center of Tom's life—baseball and basketball mostly—since he could walk and talk.

"I learned a great deal about coaching from my father before I ever played in a real game," Penders said. "I watched him teach young players, motivate them, and prepare them to be successful. He was, and always will be, my idol. He was a fearless leader who had a tremendous passion for the sports he taught. He taught me the value of hard work and integrity. He was a leader and I wanted to be just like him."

Tom Penders was the middle of three boys between Jimmy and Billy, with a younger sister, Kathy. The working-class Irish Catholic family was supported by his father's high school salary and his mother Lillian's loving care. There was a lot of horseplay and sibling rivalry. "We'd play games of Wiffle ball to the bitter end," older brother Jimmy, who later was a University of Connecticut baseball teammate, told the *Boston Globe* several years ago. "And if Tommy wasn't winning, which was often because I was older, he'd either throw the bat at me or refuse to continue the game. He wouldn't accept losing."

Tom Penders' hometown was filled with mills and other industrial-type businesses. Stratford was a tough, industrial town where boys had to become men early if they wanted to be *real* men. "If you got in a game at the boys' clubs where I grew up, you had to be tough," Tom Penders said. "There were no fouls called. It wasn't a pretty game. You had to be able to give and take and keep your mouth shut and play. And if some guy was trying to rough you up, you had better be able to stand up for yourself. If somebody wanted to pick a fight or intimidate me, I'd never back down.

"When I was real young, another kid stole my street shoes when I was playing basketball. My mother and father were not happy. And I fought him a few days later when I saw him wearing them. I developed a toughness."

Early in life, he saw how to channel that toughness on the court into the point guard position. As a player, as a coach, as a person, Tom Penders has always been on point, in the hunt, on the edge, and in the gym working to be the best point guard, and ultimately the best coach he could become.

The fact he was a coach's son was a plus, but latching onto the theory very early that the point guard was going to be his position benefited him as a college coach greatly. Just as others of his generation, such as Boston College's Jim O'Brien, Duke's Mike Krzyzewski (who played at Army), and Maryland's Gary Williams, who played and coached the Terrapins, Penders transferred a point guard mentality from the floor to the bench over the course of his career.

Who were the point guards whom Tom Penders idolized when he was growing up? First, Bob Cousy, who played at Holy Cross in the 1940s and then starred for the Boston Celtics. Johnny Egan from Hartford Weaver High School was even closer to Penders' home of Stratford. Egan later became a star at Providence and would play for six NBA teams from 1961 to 1972 and was coach of the Houston Rockets from 1973 to 1976.

"I still remember quite vividly a game that had a tremendous impact on my life and my career when I was eleven years old," Penders said. "It was March 1957, and Hartford Weaver High School played Hillhouse High of New Haven at the New Haven Arena in the state tournament. My high school, Stratford, had lost in the 7 p.m. game, and I was more than distraught. My dad had driven my little brother Billy and my older brother Jimmy and me to the arena, and they wanted me to go home because we had school the next day. I begged my dad to let us see the second game—maybe even cried. We made a compromise: We would watch the first half."

Little Tommy Penders knew that meant they probably would stay for the entire game because Egan from Hartford Weaver High was going to be displaying his skills. And playmaker Egan was viewed as the next Bob Cousy in New England, even though he was just seventeen years old.

"On this evening, Egan stole the show," Penders said. "I didn't take my eyes off him for thirty-two minutes. He was a magician with the ball. I was officially hooked after this game. I was going to be the next Johnny Egan! That game changed my life forever. From that day on basketball was an intimate part of my soul."

Penders honed his game in the Stratford schoolyards and the boys' clubs of Bridgeport and eventually became one of the best high school guards in the state of Connecticut. He was worthy of playing for the Connecticut Huskies. He led the state of Connecticut in scoring during his senior year in high school, perfecting his shot by making five hundred a day in practice every day during the entire year.

"My sophomore year at Connecticut I was a point guard who came off the bench. I was the feisty point guard," Penders added. "At one point, I got upset because I wasn't starting. I quit for one day, but I just couldn't stay away from basketball for long. It was like a drug addict without his stash. I went back the next day. And I never did think about quitting again. I think I developed into a leader on the team, even though I was coming off the bench and playing behind a guy who was older and was an Air Force veteran. My development mentally in this aspect of becoming a leader helped me later as a coach. I discovered I could contribute a lot to the team, without the glory of starting the game."

The Huskies pressed full court and ran—both styles Penders often used as a coach during his career. "I was a very poor man's Steve Nash as a college player," Penders said of averaging more than thirty minutes a game as a point guard during three varsity seasons (1964–67) under Coach Fred Shabel. Entering his senior season, Penders was labeled by *Sports Illustrated* in its college basketball preseason magazine as "a small, self-made player who has become the club leader."

"Coach Shabel had been the top assistant at Duke before coming to UConn in the spring of 1963," Penders said. "He taught the uptempo style of game that Duke and UCLA successfully employed during that era. We often pressed our opponents into submission for forty minutes a game. We ran and we usually got up more shots than our opponents, and we did not turn the ball over often. My coach would go nuts, even if we threw an errant pass in practice. I had no idea that I was going to be a basketball coach, but much of my philosophy came from my college coach. We were always in better shape than our opponents, aggressive on defense, and we ran the fast break to perfection."

Penders' boyhood dream was to play at the old Madison Square Garden. And he did once during his sophomore season (1964–65) at Connecticut. "We were pitted against Manhattan College in a doubleheader at the Garden," Penders said. "Larry Lembo, who later would become one of the top officials in college basketball, was on that Manhattan team. Notre Dame played New York University in the other game of the doubleheader.

"I was so nervous on the first shot I put up, I wouldn't even call it an air ball, I would call it a wood ball," Penders recalled. "It was so long, it hit nothing but the wood on the floor. And everybody just sort of froze and stood there; they were so shocked by the shot. But I settled down and had seventeen points, eight in overtime and we won, 80–75. After watching New York University beat Notre Dame, we came out of the Garden and the *New York Daily News* was already out with my name and my roommate's, Ron Ritter, in the headlines (for the victory)."

"Penders' shooting from the line—especially under that terrible pressure—was one of the finest exhibitions I have ever seen," Shabel said of three one-and-ones Penders made in that game.

Penders' mental toughness was matched by his physical approach to the game. During a Yankee Conference playoff game against Rhode Island to determine the league's representative to the 1966 NCAA Tournament, the six-foot, 180-pound Penders took on the Rams' burly six-foot-eight, 240-pound center Art Stephenson from the Bronx.

Stephenson grabbed a rebound, threw his elbow, and clipped Penders in the forehead. Without the referees watching, Penders threw a roundhouse right and took Stephenson's eyebrow off. Penders then took off down the floor with Stephenson in hot pursuit. Finally, Stephenson caught Penders and hit him in the back of the head, which the refs saw.

"Everybody in the building knew I had thrown a punch down at the other end and he is bleeding, but Art got thrown out of the game near the end of the first half," Penders said. "He averaged something like sixteen points, ten rebounds a game. I was a point guard. We didn't have a backup. But my coach would have let us both get thrown out and taken the trade. I remained in the game."

UConn still lost, 67–62, but Penders' legend as a feisty point guard grew. And the Rhode Island fans made a mental note of a player who one day would become their head basketball coach.

"Tommy responded very well in the responsibility of quarter-backing our basketball team," Shabel said of Penders' junior season. "We were confident that our offense is in good hands when he is directing play."

Penders doubled as a centerfielder for the Huskies' baseball team, and his brother Jim was a baseball teammate at UConn. During his senior year, Penders was captain of both teams. Baseball was the sport in which he might have continued into the pros. Penders was selected in the January 1968 Regular Phase Major League Baseball Draft by the Cleveland Indians. He was the number 116 pick (ninth round) overall and played in the Cleveland Indians' farm system that summer in Rock Hill, South Carolina (Class A), and then in Waterbury, Connecticut (AA). He was the Western Carolina (Class A) all-star third baseman from Rock Hill, where he hit .302 during his stay in South Carolina.

"I knew I could play in the major leagues," said Penders, who played in both the NCAA Tournament and College World Series when he was a sophomore in 1965. "And I thought if I hung in there another three or four years, I definitely could have made the major leagues."

Penders' Connecticut baseball coach Larry Panciera told the *Hartford Courant*, "I've never seen any fellow with his confidence. Why Tommy could go right out today and play centerfield for the Yankees—and it would not bother him a bit. The fact he might strike out four times and drop a ball in the outfield wouldn't shake his confidence at all."

But high school basketball coaching was beckoning him back to Connecticut.

"We roomed together," said Rick Schwartz, a minor-league teammate of Penders that summer and a now-retired news director for Fox Sports Network. "He told me that he was quitting baseball and going to coach high school basketball. I said, 'What are you, nuts?' He was a very, very good baseball player, and he could hit and he had ferociousness in his own way and gumption to do it. I said, 'You are nuts to coach high school basketball. You have to stay with baseball for awhile.'"

But Penders had aspirations of moving up the coaching ladder, which he did very quickly. In only three total seasons, he turned around programs at Bullard Havens Technical and Bridgeport Central, and was on his way to Tufts.

COACHING LIKE A POINT GUARD

Penders always went back to his point guard experience during his intriguing coaching journey. He often had some of the best point guards in the country, sometimes multiple ones.

At Penders' second college stop and first Division I school, Columbia, the diminutive, five-foot-seven Alton Byrd was a magician with the ball. "There was no shot clock nor three-point line in the mid-1970s, so you had a chance to hang close to the power teams if you had great guards who could control the game," Penders said. "Alton Byrd could dominate the tempo of any game. He was a coach on the floor. Alton did not need my help in running the offense. In today's games, point guards are rare if they can run an offense until they are juniors or seniors."

Byrd had yet to arrive on campus during Penders' first season at Columbia in 1974–75 when the Lions were on their way to a 4–22 record. In fact, Penders knew nothing of Byrd before a chance meeting at Madison Square Garden with Golden State Warriors coach Al Attles.

Early during Penders' first season, Columbia had a game against Fordham at Madison Square Garden and practiced back-to-back with the Golden State Warriors one day. Penders was introduced to Attles. "I told him I had a couple of Bay Area kids on my team," Penders recalled. "He told me there is a great little point guard out in San Francisco that Phil Smith (Warriors shooting guard) plays with all summer long. He calls Phil over and said, 'Tell coach about Alton Byrd.' He told me Byrd was a playground legend. I asked, 'How are his grades?' And he said, 'He is a really smart kid. Stanford is recruiting him. And so is Santa Clara.'"

Penders had another kid from the same Riordan High School already on his team: Elmer Love, a freshman. When Love was asked why he hadn't mentioned Byrd, Love told Penders he believed Byrd was going to stay home and go to Stanford. Penders started recruiting him and Byrd changed his mind.

During Byrd's sophomore season at Columbia, Penders' third year at the school, he became a force after sitting out because of freshman ineligibility rules in the Ivy League. Early that season the Lions traveled to nearby Rutgers, which had made the 1976 Final

Four the previous season. Eddie Jordan and James Bailey, who both later played in the NBA, led the Scarlet Knights. Rutgers had not lost at home in two seasons.

"We ran a four-corner-type offense when we got the lead, and we ended up beating them 85–75," Penders recalled. "Alton made a play where he was out in the middle of the floor, and Eddie came out, who was lightening quick himself, and tried to get a five-count on Alton. He dribbled the ball between Eddie's legs and went around him and drove to the basket. James Bailey went over to block Alton's layup and Alton threw a behind-the-back pass to Shane Cotner, who maybe had the only dunk of his career."

Said Byrd, "From that stage, we controlled the rest of the game. I think the Rutgers fans were somewhat shocked. They thought we were cannon fodder as most Ivy teams were when they played teams in the East back then."

Later, Byrd, a three-time All-Ivy League selection, became one of the first scoring point guards in European professional basketball.

"There was more of a stigma for small players back then than there is now," Byrd said. "It was different. There was no three-point line. The point guard had a lot more of a role in terms of control. People had this, 'He's too small.' I kind of saw myself as one of the earlier pilgrims, not only here, but in Europe. I was one of the first guards to get paid to play in Europe. Usually they would have two American players, and they were big guys. Once I got to Europe, I was asked to not only score, but pass, control tempo, and create opportunities, and defend."

A professional basketball star in England and Scotland after playing at Columbia, Byrd has become a successful businessman abroad and in the United States and currently runs a San Francisco–based company that markets and manages events and promotions.

FROM FORDHAM TO HOUSTON: POINT GUARDS GALORE

At Fordham, Jerry Hobbie and Tony McIntosh provided some of the leadership for five National Invitation Tournament bids during Penders' seasons there.

"McIntosh and Hobbie at Fordham were not spectacular players, but they were great shooters, great free throw shooters, and never turned the ball over," Penders said. "They were All-Conference. But we never got to the NCAA Tournament, so they never developed national names."

Then at Rhode Island for two seasons in 1986–88, Penders virtually had two point guards with Carlton "Silk" Owens and Tom Garrick. The Rams made a run in the NCAA Tournament in 1988. But one regular-season play stood out during those two seasons. "We were playing on ESPN on Martin Luther King Day against George Washington, and other than Ernie DiGregorio's seventy-five-foot bounce pass against Memphis State in the 1973 Final Four semifinals, it was the best pass I have ever seen," Penders said. "We got the outlet to Silk, and Tommy Garrick was flying down the court. Silk threw a bounce pass that went right between a GW player's legs. Garrick caught it and laid it up and in. Silk Owens could pass off the dribble. He was a lefty, without putting his right hand on the ball better than any player I have ever seen.

"Garrick and Owens were an incredibly efficient and smart duo. Owens may have been the greatest point guard whom I ever coached. Garrick was a relentless scorer and great defender."

During his years at Texas, Penders played three guards most of the time, with some interchangeable at the point guard spot—Travis Mays, Joey Wright, and Lance Blanks from 1988 to 1990. Mays and Blanks both wound up being drafted as point guards in the first round of the 1990 NBA Draft.

"I had the most fun in basketball playing with those two guys," Blanks said. "That three-guard offense, everyone could play anywhere on the perimeter. Basically we would run, shoot, and put pressure on the other team. I remember during some of the first practices, I would pass up a shot and he (Penders) would say, 'If you pass up shots like that you will be sitting by me over on the sidelines.' The system was built to score, get up and down the floor, put pressure on the defense, taking threes, and keeping the floor spread."

A few years later at Texas, Penders instituted another revolving attack with B. J. Tyler, Terrence Rencher, and Roderick Anderson. They all played together during the second half of the 1993–94 season when Texas won the second of three regular-season Southwest Conference (SWC) titles under Penders. Penders won his first SWC post-season tournament championship that season as well.

"B. J. missed most of the first semester, so we needed another guard to go along with Rencher to replace him until he got back," Penders said of Tyler's suspension.

"I convinced Roderick (a junior college transfer) when B. J. got back that all three could play together. It didn't bother me to have two point guards out there at the same time. My philosophy has always been if you have two point guards out there, you have two great decision makers. But they have to be able to score to play them together. Roderick said about the situation, 'Well, I will either beat B. J. out, or he will learn to play with me.' That's the kind of confidence he had. We were pretty lethal that year. That was my best overall team at Texas."

At his next two stops, George Washington and Houston, Penders had numerous good guards, either point or combination thereof. At George Washington, the five-foot-three, 155-pound Shawnta

Rogers dazzled Atlantic 10 teams with his steals, assists, and scoring. "He was one of the best players in the country," Penders said. At Houston, Lanny Smith, Zamal Nixon, and Desmond Wade all stood out as point guards in Penders' turnaround of the Cougars, who had suffered nine losing seasons in the previous eleven before his arrival.

Thinking like a point guard, Penders believes he had an advantage over coaches who really hadn't been in the heat of battle in big-time college games. "I have a very strong belief that coaches who have played college basketball at the very highest level have an edge over those who have not played at a very high level or those who may not have even played college basketball." Penders said. "I think it's a lot easier to understand the psyche of players and pressure under which they perform and to be more analytical when you have played. You don't get caught up in the distractions that can fall into place.

"On the day of a game I can take a call from a sportswriter or be on a radio show, because when that show is over, my focus is right back on what I am going to do. I don't need eight hours on the day of the game to prepare. I review things, take a few notes, and think about things that could happen and what I should adjust to. But most of my adjustments are made on the fly from recalling experiences I had as a player.

"I don't see how a guy who was just a manager or the last man on the bench could have that kind of understanding. It is like being at the throttle, being a pilot of an airplane versus someone passing out coffee like a flight attendant. Yeah, they have been on the airplane. They know certain safety features. And they know the dangers of flying. But how confident would you be as a passenger to let this flight attendant control the airplane? Imagine someone coaching his first year and never having played. What did his stomach feel like?

How many times did he throw up? I have never been sick before a game because of nerves."

Penders said he could always tell when he was pitted against another coach who had played college basketball, especially guys who were guards: Krzyzewski, Williams, O'Brien, former DePaul coach Joey Meyer, former Boston College coach Al Skinner, and Louisville coach Rick Pitino. The latter two both starred at UMass during their playing days.

"When you coached against Lon Kruger and came up with something new, you had to save it until the second half," Penders said of the current University of Nevada–Las Vegas head coach who was a guard at Kansas State. "If you did something in the first half, at halftime he would make all the adjustments and rip the same defense because he had played the game. You don't out-coach Jim Boeheim. He was a great college player at Syracuse. He was six foot six, but when he had the ball, he played like a point guard."

Penders said he studies point guards on the opposing teams. "When I scout a game I watch the point guard dribble by dribble, pass by pass," Penders added. "He's the guy I watch the most. How important is he? How smart is he? Does he tip off what they do? Or is he one of those guys no matter what you do to him he is going to make the right decision on his own? That has a lot to do with your strategy."

When Penders was coach at the University of Texas, his Longhorns faced Oklahoma State during the 1997–98 season when the Cowboys had first-year point guard Doug Gottlieb, who led the country with 8.8 assists a game the following season. Although Texas struggled in 1997–98, Penders' final season at Texas, the Longhorns beat the NCAA Tournament–bound Cowboys two out of three games.

"Doug would absolutely pick you apart if you played him straight up. But if you laid off him and made him the guy to beat you (scoring), he struggled," Penders said. "That's because I studied Doug. Texas was the only school who played him that way. In Big 12 play, I played him with my worst defender, who was six foot eight or six foot nine, and would make him beat us. Doug had a great college career and would make a fine coach himself. It's just when he played against the University of Texas, I knew and respected how good he was, but I had played the position and discovered his weaknesses. He was a 'pass first' point guard so we dared him to shoot and fouled him as soon as they were in the bonus foul situation. Doug might make one of the two foul shots, but rarely went two for two. We fouled him whether we were up six or down ten. It always worked. I was 5–1 (career) against Oklahoma State and four of those came against Eddie Sutton, one of the sport's greatest coaching legends. You don't outcoach Eddie Sutton. Your players make shots and respect what the other team does well. You penetrate, kick it out, and knock down your open shots. I had the utmost respect for an Eddie Sutton–coached team."

OFFICIALS:

A GAME WITHIN A GAME

"Every game is like a painting, and the painting can look like a masterpiece or a mess, depending on the people who control the ebb and flow of the game. Show me a great game, and I'll show you a well-officiated game."

—Tom Penders

Texas coach Tom Penders took to the podium after a semifinal game of the 1990 Southwest Conference (SWC) Post-Season Tournament at Reunion Arena. After a contest against Houston that had about as much excitement as a taffy pull because of sixty-four free throws shot between the two teams, Penders was livid at the game officials. Houston shot twenty more free throws than Penders' Longhorns.

"If you want a circus, put a tent over it," said Penders, who received three technical fouls for complaining about the officiating and was ejected in the Longhorns' 89–86 loss. Texas' star senior guard, Travis Mays, playing in his last SWC game, also chimed in about the officiating. He said it was probably the worst he had ever seen.

Mays was lucky—he was headed to the NBA after the season and never again would have to face SWC referees. Penders had to return to the SWC for many more seasons of officiating fun and games—but only after he sat out the Longhorns' SWC opener the following January against Texas A&M in Austin. A one-game suspension was handed down by the league office for Penders' "tent" comments.

The 1989–90 season was one of the most tumultuous yet flamboyant in SWC history, with officiating controversies galore. Several of the incidents involved Penders or his players, who were trying to bring a frenetically paced style to the Southwest hardwoods to compete with the Arkansas Razorbacks, coached by Nolan Richardson.

During the 1989–90 season, Penders and Richardson were involved in one of the most talked-about games in SWC history when Richardson walked off the court near the end of regulation in a game in Austin. Richardson received no technical foul for walking out of the coaching box. Arkansas tied the score on a last-second shot, and the game went into overtime (with Richardson returning to the bench) where the Razorbacks won the controversy-tinged game, 103–96.

"After the game, Mike Tanco, one of the SWC officials, said a coach could walk away from the bench during the game and not receive a technical foul," Penders said. Later, Ed Steitz, NCAA secretary rules editor, announced that SWC officials erred in not giving Richardson a technical foul.

Later in the season, Penders had a runway run-in with Tanco after a game in which UT guard Joey Wright said Tanco told him to shut up. "I am not indicting Mike's integrity or character, but he was never in a good mood and seemed to think that the fans were there to see him put on a show," Penders said. "He had a good career and I believe that he could have been one of the best if he could have checked his ego at the entrance door. He was a negative role model for young officials because of his combative manner, even though he could officiate."

Penders said he believed SWC officials were going to show him, an Easterner, "how the game was called down here."

"The referees would call touch fouls, traveling when there was no traveling, and they didn't understand the jump stop," said Penders, whose teams would play aggressive defense trying to steal the ball and pick up the touch fouls. "The referees back in the East understood the jump stop. It was not traveling. When I came down here, I had to put on clinics and have our players demonstrate to officials before the game."

Recently, Shaquille O'Neal, who went to high school in San Antonio and played against Penders' Texas teams when he was a college star at LSU, gave credit to Penders. NBA veteran O'Neal, now a member of the Boston Celtics, told the *Boston Herald*, "Tom Penders taught me the jump stop. I used to do that move in college and when I first got to the league (NBA), the refs didn't know what it was, so they used to call a travel all the time. But, yeah, Tom Penders is my guy. I almost went to Texas, but it was too close to the crib.

"I had to get away. One hour and six hours is a big (expletive) difference. Texas was there, but it was just too close. But Tom Penders is one of the people who really helped me."

Penders remembers his struggles teaching the jump stop to officials in Texas and points beyond. "David Hall, who was a great referee, would be in my all-time top ten. David is from Denver. And I remember him coming over to me and asking, 'Coach can you have a couple of your players come over?' 'I want to study this jump stop before a game.' So I had Joey Wright and Travis Mays go over there, and he'd look at it. And I said, 'The whole key to it, David, is when the guy is about to make that last big step he doesn't have both hands on the ball. In other words, his dribble hasn't really stopped yet, and he is starting to make that step and now when he brings both hands up, he has started that last hop.' He said, 'Okay, that makes sense.'

Gradually, the refs caught on to it."

After the 1990–91 season, the SWC released several game officials and following the 1992–93 season, the supervisor of officials was gone when the last SWC commissioner Steve Hatchell, on one of his first days on the job, watched a technical-infested, foul-frenzied, quarterfinal round of games in the SWC Post-Season Tournament. Texas A&M radio announcer Dave South was even ejected by a SWC official from an Aggie–Houston game after making a "choke" sign to game official Bryan Stout by grabbing his throat with his hands. During another game later that day, a Baylor trainer picked up a technical.

"This type of thing was common in SWC games, but it was hard to believe that it was happening in front of Hatchell," Penders said. "It was truly a circus, and it really hurt the quality of the game in the SWC."

Unlike three years previous, Penders didn't have to make any "tent" comments that day in a press conference. Following the A&M–Houston game, an astonished Hatchell sprinted down the hall by the UT dressing room after watching the spectacle of SWC officiating and exclaimed, "How in the world did you put up with this all these years!?"

Penders responded, "Steve, I guess you have not been reading the newspapers because I've been doing the best I can to change things, but it's up to you and the conference office to do something about it. The coaches can't do anything about this."

Shortly after the tournament, Hatchell fired the SWC supervisor of officials, Paul Galvan, and replaced him with Dale Kelly, who turned around the situation.

Over the years, regardless of the league in which he has coached, Penders believes the game was constantly changing and the officials had to keep up with those changes. "The athletes get better and better, and the coaching tries to keep up with the players and so, too, do the officials," Penders said. "The speed of the game gets faster every year, and officials have to keep up, blend in, and keep reasonable control of the game without over whistling and breaking the flow. Calls are going to be missed and focus must be kept by every person that's part of the action. So many things occur in rapid motion. And it takes so many qualities and abilities by the officials to keep control while allowing the players and coaches to determine the outcome of the game. These refs have to be in great shape mentally and physically."

ACC REFS TO THE RESCUE

At Texas, Penders would bring in Atlantic Coast Conference officials to do his big non-conference games. "I was so disappointed with SWC refs that after my first year, when I would contract games against such schools as Connecticut, North Carolina, and Florida, I worked out a deal with Fred Barakat (the ACC supervisor of officials)," Penders said. "In any of our non-conference games, we would use ACC refs. It was better to have neutral refs because it took all the pressure off the referees. There is a tremendous amount of pressure on referees when they represent the Southeastern Conference when they are working, say, the Florida–Houston game. The SEC is a desired conference for them to officiate games in. They are going to lean toward the conference they work for. It's only natural these refs don't want to upset the coaches from the power conferences."

When using ACC referees, Penders even pulled one over on University of Texas at El Paso (UTEP) coach Don Haskins during the 1994–95 season in the four-team Sun Carnival Classic played on the Miners' home floor in El Paso. "I only agreed to play in the tournament if our games were worked by ACC refs," Penders said with a chuckle. "Don Haskins didn't know anything about it. Craig Helwig was the head of the Sun Bowl at that time, and he was a former associate athletic director at Texas and wanted Texas in the tournament. It just so happened we played North Carolina in the Sun Bowl that year in football, so we also had a great turnout of Texas fans.

"Haskins went nuts when he found out about it, and UTEP fans were all over me. They booed me as soon as my name was announced. I said we didn't want to go down there and have Western Athletic Conference officials, the conference UTEP was in at the time."

As it turned out Texas didn't play UTEP, which was upset in the first round by Washington State. Texas beat Texas–Pan American in the first round, then Washington State for the title. "I am not saying ACC officials would have favored us (in a game against UTEP)," Penders said, "but they wouldn't have given the Bear the edge he usually got when you went into the Don Haskins Center. I just wanted neutral officials, and the ACC had the very best."

"In my first seventeen years as a college coach (before Texas), I had very few problems with officials," Penders said. "I am not saying that I was a choirboy on the sidelines, but the officials I came into contact with were the top guys in the country—NCAA Tournament–level officials. I always felt like I had a great relationship with officials, and when I got to the NCAA Tournament most of the officials knew me."

HOW THE NCAA BASKETBALL OFFICIALS ARE ADMINISTERED

College basketball has had three key national rules and officiating figures during Tom Penders' nearly four decades of coaching: Ed Steitz, Hank Nichols, and now John Adams.

Ed Steitz served as the national rules interpreter for the first twenty or so years of Penders' coaching career. He was once the basketball coach, then later athletic director, at Springfield (Massachusetts) College. From 1965 to 1990, he worked for the NCAA Men's Basketball Rules Committee as a secretary, editor, and national interpreter of rules. "He was known to make public comments about poor officiating often after nationally televised games," Penders said. "He tried his best to bring accountability from the officiating side of things, but for most of his tenure television had nowhere near the coverage it has today. His main job came in March when he assigned officials to work the NCAA Tournament. It didn't matter who you were, if you had a bad performance or blew a key call you were finished for the rest of March Madness. Reputation meant very little to Ed Steitz, who tried very hard to have the game called the same in all parts of the country; but there were wide differences in every pocket of the nation."

Hank Nichols, who officiated in six NCAA title games, became the NCAA's national coordinator of men's basketball officials in 1986, a new position. He took over many of Steitz's duties and held that title through 2008. Nichols was also a professor at Villanova University for many years. "Hank was a super official and worked many of my games," Penders said. "He was a man of integrity, who had the skills and intangibles that allowed him to be one of the best ever to officiate. I always loved to see Hank Nichols show up when we played road games. He was thick skinned and never got intimidated by an unruly crowd. Except to say 'nice call,' you never even tried to get to Hank because it was useless to try. Hank was not going to be influenced by anything. As far as I know Hank had the utmost respect of every college coach that ever had him work a game or saw him officiate. He took charge without anybody noticing.

"But, in my opinion, Hank was too quiet as a supervisor and didn't have the visibility or the desire to control the national scene the way that Ed Steitz did," Penders added. "During the season you never saw or heard from Hank, and most officials will say the same thing. Too many officials were doing their own thing, and nobody was seemingly in control during Hank's watch."

In 2008, John Adams took over as the new NCAA national coordinator of officials. He's strong, demanding, very candid, and visible. He seems to be everywhere and certainly available to talk to coaches and officials from all over the country. Adams, a former college basketball official, had been coordinator of men's basketball officiating for the Horizon League for a decade before taking the NCAA post.

"If an official isn't in great physical condition or has a bad attitude he will be in trouble with John Adams," Penders said. "John seems to have a great passion for the game and an understanding of what coaches are up against. Hopefully, he'll be able to bring everything involving officiating into his shop, but the NCAA has got to grant him the power, or accountability will never become a reality.

"Officials are people who come from a variety of backgrounds. While they are independent contractors they also need rules, regulations, and direction. Every league in the country has a supervisor of officials, but that person isn't really under the control of the national supervisor. He answers to his conference office. And many conferences don't have a clue about officiating. Until every conference supervisor is held accountable to the national supervisor, the system will never be what it should be. The NBA has one supervisor whose job status depends on how good his officials are. That is not quite the way it works in college, but it is getting better."

Penders would like to see more transparency by Adams and the NCAA regarding how officials advance in the NCAA Tournament. Every Division I conference sends at least two of their best officials to the NCAA Tournament. "They supposedly advance by performance, though I'm not 100 percent sure that some don't advance by reputation," Penders said. "It's an area that needs more transparency. People, especially coaches, should know how or why officials advance to the Final Four or Sweet 16. I'd like to see all officials advance by performance and with each advance their paycheck should double. You would see some real focus when they get to that $5,000 game or the game that leads to the big payday. Competition usually brings out the best in all of us."

This might help in another area. The NBA had a huge scare with the recent point shaving and betting scandal with an official, Tim Donaghy, who bet on NBA games and controlled the outcome. And strong rumors have circulated that there could be similar problems with officials in college basketball.

One of those rumors is that a high-level official might have been a bookie before he entered the ranks of college basketball officiating. If this is true, it could shake the college game at least as much as Donaghy did to the NBA just from appearance sake. Penders acknowledged, "This rumor was floating around amongst coaches over the last five years, and I trust that the rumor is only a rumor. I believe that everybody deserves second chances, even bookies. We all do dumb things when we are young, and coaches are not always choirboys either. I was born in Bridgeport, Connecticut, and sports betting was part of everyday life there. I played semi-professional basketball and baseball, and our team was sponsored by the biggest bookie in Bridgeport. He was a great man who was loved in our community. I don't think he bet on our games, however."

"Coaches are paranoid about officials to begin with," Penders said, "and I personally have a dislike for any official who constantly looks at the scoreboard, because officials should focus on the action on the floor, the coaches, and the shot clock, which is on the top of the backboard. When an official looks at the scoreboard coaches think he is looking for fouls (individual or team). It is just natural for a coach to feel that way. If there is a malfunction on the big clock, the clock operator and the game operations people are in control and are supposed to oversee that, not the officials on the floor working the game.

"We all pray that it never happens in college basketball, but the temptation and money will always be there for people with a lack of passion for the game or a sense of sociopathic entitlement. Officials are underpaid, independent contractors. The top fifty coaches are making a million or more per year. Top officials earn maybe $50,000 to $110,000 a year. One can only guess what motivates an official to cheat. Strong leadership can make the possibility of such a scandal even more remote. There never will be a bulletproof system, but background checks and strong, powerful leadership are a deterrent for anyone who is tempted to abuse the system. Coaches make too much money to even think about messing with gambling. Officials don't make a lot of money, and they should be paid more because they are critical for the success of the sport.

"Nobody can police people for twenty-four seven, fifty-two weeks a year, but the game is too important to ignore the conduct of anyone involved with the sport. A tough and experienced person has to be in control. And I believe that college basketball officiating will continue to improve under John Adams's watch."

THE BEST OFFICIALS HAVE GOOD ATTITUDES

Penders said he has never been able to tolerate officials who have poor attitudes and who have been openly confrontational with coaches and players. "If a referee is showy or colorful that's fine with me, but there is never an excuse for an official to show up for a game with a negative attitude, no matter how many games he has worked in the last month," Penders said. "Some of the greatest officials have been very confident and colorful types and some you barely notice, but if they are competent and have a positive attitude, that's all that you can expect.

"I strongly believe that coaches and officials need to know and trust each other as much as possible. Back in my New York City years it was common for coaches and officials to all meet at the same restaurant after doubleheaders at Madison Square Garden. We got to know and trust each other. Officials and coaches would even sit together at awards banquets and play in charity golf tournaments together. Officials would be invited to coaches' meetings and coaches would be invited to speak at officials' meetings. Nobody gained an advantage, and every coach knew every official and officials developed a feel for the coaches. The game needs that. It's not like the NBA where coaches and NBA officials work everyone's games on a regular basis, and they often bump into one another. They develop a rapport with the coaches, all coaches. I know many NBA coaches, and they trust NBA officials with very few exceptions. That trust needs to be there in the college game."

Here are some of the best officials who have officiated Penders' games over the years (some are retired or no longer with us): Jimmy Howell, Hank Nichols, Pete Pavia, Irv Brown, Jim Bain, David Hall, Mickey Crowley, Gerry Donaghy, Jim Burr, Tim Higgins, Lynn Shortnacy, John Clougherty, Booker Turner, Dick Paparo, Tom O'Neill, Curtis Shaw, Steve Welmer, Ed Hightower, Verne Harris, John Higgins, Bryan Kersey, Bill Kennedy, Brent Barnaky, Lee Cassell, Duke Edsall, Doug Sirmons, and Doug Shows.

"Over the years I have made some lasting friendships with college basketball officials," Penders said. "There are some great people in the business. My father was a basketball official for many years and also served as a supervisor after he hung up his whistle. He loved the game, and he was respected by everyone.

"Pete Pavia was a dear friend of mine for over twenty years. I battled his cancer with him for what seemed like an eternity. He never gave me a call during a game, and I didn't expect one. We never talked about the particulars of a call or a game of mine.

"When he came to New York to work a St. John's versus Georgetown game we would try to hook up for dinner. We talked about the games, and he had a great attitude about the game and the players and coaches. He always said that he worked for the players and the coaches. He gave you the best effort he had. I coached every practice for over fifteen years with Pete Pavia's name engraved on my whistle. It was a daily reminder of what a great friend he was. I will have it encased with all of my memorabilia for the rest of my life. It's just as important to me as a championship watch or ring because it allows me to think of my good friend Pete."

Pavia finally lost his battle against cancer in 1992. He worked his last Final Four in 1991 at the Hoosier Dome in Indianapolis in a semifinal game between Kansas and North Carolina. Tar Heels coach Dean Smith, who had picked up an earlier technical, received two additional technical fouls from Pavia with thirty-five seconds remaining on the way to a 79–73 NCAA semifinal loss to the Jayhawks.

Smith said something to Pavia when a foul was called on North Carolina player Rick Fox, who fouled out of the game. Smith received another technical foul (his third in the game), when he was deemed to be out of the coaching box, and was ejected.

"I asked Pete many times what was said, and he said that he had too much respect for Dean Smith to even let his wife Debbie know what was said," Penders said. "Pete just smiled whenever I asked. He was just too classy to say something and appear to be showing up a coach. Other officials might brag about such things, but not Pete."

TOM PENDERS' GUIDE TO GOOD OFFICIATING

The keys to being a good college basketball official and part of the three-man crew:

1. Never, ever let a crowd influence your calls.

2. Be consistent as a crew, not just individually. You must communicate before and during games.

3. Never let a coach buy a call or technical foul by his acting out on the sidelines.

4. It's sometimes good to be hard of hearing, but it's never good to be blind.

5. Communicate respectfully with coaches and players and never accept disrespect from them.

6. Until you have really established yourself, try to avoid calling technical fouls.

7. If you have to call a technical foul, call it—don't look back and don't flaunt it.

8. Strive for consistency throughout the game with your partners. Know what's going on in the game.

9. Never carry a grudge toward a coach or player. Forget and move on.

10. The best officials blend in well and never try to be the show.

11. Call it like you see it. If you are good, you will last a long time in the game. It's all about survival.

12. Hand-checking is too prevalent and is hurting the college game. Call it and the players will adjust and coaches will stop teaching it.

DEAD PROGRAMS RISING

"It's not just about wins and losses or about gaudy records. It is about survival. How many coaches have survived Tufts?"

—Tom Penders on his college coaching career that started at Tufts

During Tom Penders' thirty-six-year college career, he coached at seven different schools, six on the Division I level. No other coach in the history of the game has coached at more Division I schools, and only four others have coached as many as seven schools on any level.

Penders' trail from Tufts in the early 1970s all the way to Houston in the new millennium was wrought with difficult rebuilding jobs at all the stops early in his career (Tufts, Columbia, Fordham, Rhode Island, and Texas). In each of the first four cases, the programs had single-digit victory totals the season before Penders arrived. Basically, they were dead.

"Even when I went to Texas, they had had low attendance and there was no expectation level," Penders said of the spring of 1988. "But it was the University of Texas. I was brought in there to at least make them respectable and sell some tickets and get them on television. I never in my pre-Texas years ever saw them on a nationally televised game. I didn't know what the ceiling was at Texas when I went there.

"I knew what the ceilings were at the other schools. You don't go to Fordham University, for instance, expecting to be a regular participant in the NCAA Tournament. At your very highest hope, you are thinking of a possible NIT berth. Take a twenty-game loser and turn it into an eighteen- or twenty-game winner was about as far as you could go. You have to be realistic about that when you decide to make a move."

Penders always subscribed to this axiom during his coaching career at the seven different stops. "I would say a coach who doesn't coach around his talent and abilities of his players will not be around very long," Penders said. "It's not like the NBA where you can set a style and then draft or trade to your needs. The commitment your school makes to the basketball program will dictate your talent. There are ten to fifteen schools in the country—such as Kentucky, North Carolina, and Kansas—that get to choose their players. There are other schools from the power conferences who also have their pick of players. Talent is key, but just getting talent doesn't mean a coach will hang on for a lengthy career. He needs to get the most out of it and also adjust to the players' strengths and weaknesses."

Penders' son, Tommy, who played for his father at Texas in the mid-1990s and later was an assistant coach for him at George Washington, stressed that the key to his father's longevity as a coach was his ability to relate to his players throughout the decades. "Without a doubt, it is his ability to relate to a player in the 1970s, 1980s, 1990s, 2000s. Kids today are a lot different than kids in the 1970s. In the 1970s and into the 1980s, he was a hard-nosed disciplinarian, but by the 1990s, my father was far less demanding. Instead of calling out a player in front of the team, Dad would pull him aside or meet with the player after practice. A lot of people thought we were free-spirited (at Texas), but he ran a tight ship, just in a different way than in the 1970s and 1980s. That is his greatest strength, no doubt"

TUFTS UNIVERSITY (THREE SEASONS: 1971-74)

Penders, the head coach at Bridgeport Central (Conn.) High School in 1970–71, was twenty-five years old when he took a cut in pay to become the coach of the Tufts Jumbos. Tufts was coming off a 1–17 record in 1970–71 when Penders arrived at the then-small liberal arts college in Medford, Massachusetts, a suburb of Boston.

"I knew it was a low-pressure job. If I just got to be a .500 coach it would be looked upon as a major accomplishment," Penders said. "Although it has since changed at Tufts, at the time we weren't allowed to play for national championships. We were in a league called New England Small College Athletic Conference (NESCAC) with schools such as Amherst and Bates."

Penders' recruiting budget at Tufts was non-existent: basically written materials about the school, the basketball program, and a phone credit card. He was not allowed to recruit off campus unless it was at a university function. So he would go to the admissions office and beg for functions in Hartford and New Haven or in New York City, where he could mingle with admissions staff and prominent alumni and invite prospective basketball players to the receptions.

When he signed on at Tufts, Penders had a one-year, one-page contract worth $11,000, and his assistant Sam Bryant, a football player, received a scholarship to help Penders with the varsity Jumbos and coach the freshman basketball team. Bryant had a handshake with the Tufts athletic director Harry Arlanson. "Sam was a great guy who helped me keep the players in line," Penders said. "In the early 1970s maintaining discipline was crucial. It was a volatile period with the Vietnam War coming to a close and racial struggles popping up every day. There was always a march or a protest. I lived on campus and so did Sam. Our players were very active in campus politics, and so were we. We stuck together and even protested as a team. Those were wild times, but Sam helped me keep the ship steady."

Penders' first team at Tufts in 1971–72 went 12–8 and the Jumbos were named the "Most Improved Team in New England" after the season. Penders was quoted by the *Tufts Journal* saying, "I am honored, but I hope we never have to accept this award again." Penders never did.

Penders' next two teams posted back-to-back twenty-victory seasons in 1972–73 (22–4) and 1973–74 (20–6). The twenty-two victories were the most in Tufts history until the 2005–06 team registered twenty-three victories. The 1972–73 team had a familiar name on the squad, point guard Eddie Tapscott, who much later would become interim head coach of the Washington Wizards of the NBA and also served stints in the front offices of that franchise, the Charlotte Bobcats, and the New York Knicks. He is currently in the front office of the Washington Wizards. The 1972–73 Tufts team was inducted into the New England Basketball Hall of Fame in 2005.

Penders' back-to-back twenty-victory seasons are still the only time in Tufts' history this has occurred, through the 2009–10 season. And that accomplishment was enough to catch the eye of Columbia officials, whose program was in the bottom half of the Ivy League. Interestingly, it came down to Jim Valvano, then head coach at Johns Hopkins, and Penders for the job, and Penders won out. He asked for a $30,000-a-year salary and told Columbia officials that he could pay no more than $800 a month for housing and parking in New York City. He got both.

"I had to make the move or I would have died at Tufts," Penders said of the obvious limitations. "Some of my players at Tufts are my very best friends today. They were all smarter than me and most of them have had wonderful careers. They are all very proud of what we achieved on the court."

Another bonus of coaching at Tufts: Penders took advantage of his proximity to the Boston Celtics, one of the most successful franchises in NBA history. "During those three years at Tufts, I saw many Boston Celtic games and practices. I studied their style inside and out. They ran at every opportunity, and they did not make careless turnovers. I spent many hours listening to the great Red Auerbach, perhaps the greatest all-time coach in any sport, and the greatest motivator who ever put a whistle around his neck.

"He made absolute sense to me. He said the game was simple and coaches often complicate things. To paraphrase, 'Be unpredictable so other coaches won't know what you are doing and your players don't think they have you figured out. Find out what your players are good at and let them do it. Believe in them and explain which shots are good shots for them and don't yank them when they miss the "good shot.""

COLUMBIA (FOUR SEASONS: 1974-78)

Penders inherited a Columbia program which had been mired in the Ivy League's second division for the three previous seasons and had lost fifty-eight total games during that period, nearly twenty a season. Princeton and the University of Pennsylvania were the dominant programs in the league. Columbia had last won the Ivy League in 1968 and went to the NCAA Tournament that season, but that was the first time since 1951.

Before he even turned twenty-nine, Penders was the head coach of a Division I program. "I thought if I could somehow get up near Penn and Princeton, I had to get out of there," Penders said. "I knew the prospects of going to an NCAA Tournament at Columbia weren't good, because only the winner of the conference was going to get to go. They had a pecking order in the Ivy League. If you were a basketball player you chose Penn or Princeton. If you were academically oriented first and basketball second they had the 'H-Y-P syndrome.' Harvard, Yale, and Princeton were the three top academic schools in the Ivy League. So you were fighting two different battles."

When Penders first arrived, Columbia was moving out of an old-fashioned pillared gym that had been built in 1901 and seated just 1,700 fans. The new gym, without the obstruction of pillars, would seat 3,400. But that was still way below the seating capacities at Penn (8,722-seat Palestra) and Princeton (6,854-seat Jadwin Gymnasium).

"There were bleachers on both sides and walls on both ends," Penders said of Columbia's new basketball facility at the time. "It was a big high school gym. There are probably thirty or forty bigger high school gyms in the state of Texas. And it was in Harlem, which made it a little bit more difficult to recruit. You had to recruit city kids, not necessarily from New York City."

Jack Rohan, Columbia's coach before Penders, had made a decision to recruit in the San Francisco–Oakland area. So Penders, because it was too late to bring in new applicants to the Ivy League, followed through with those recruits and continued to develop contacts in that area, which eventually helped him land top point guard

Alton Byrd out of San Francisco. He also brought in other solid players from Midwestern cities such as Kansas City and St. Louis and one great player from the New York City area—Ricky Free from Boys and Girls High School in Brooklyn.

"Ricky Free was the only local player I had at Columbia who could really play," Penders said. "In those days, it was almost impossible to get a New York City player to stay at home and go to school. But I recruited the best player in New York City because he wanted to be close to his mother and family, and we were able to get him a great job on Wall Street. He saved his money and never had to pay for plane fare to get home. He helped his family and saved a lot of his summer earnings for his own bank account.

"If your school is in or near a rough area or in a city, it often makes it tougher to get local players. Kids want to get out of tough surroundings. They often want to get away from tough conditions at home. They don't necessarily want to be supporting their families with their Pell Grants. They often want to get away from their 'home boys' so that they have a chance to study and breathe."

Much as he did at Tufts, Penders latched on to resources outside the athletic department to help with recruiting at Columbia. He worked with the Columbia admissions office to help defray recruiting expenses and also utilized the fact he was traveling all over the country during the summers as a player on the powerhouse Raybestos Fast-Pitch Softball Team. He would visit top academic students at schools and then would see a basketball prospect. As an example, when he went to DeSmet Jesuit in St. Louis, he not only saw basketball recruit Jeff Combs, he talked to four or five other top students. His annual recruiting budget was around $5,000 at Columbia and he often went deep into his own credit card in order to recruit.

"We had eight guys my sophomore year (1976–77) from out of state and four were from California," Alton Byrd said. "In order to turn around the program, he had to do something that was non-traditional. We all came from good academic schools and he felt we could all survive the rigors of Ivy League education with no favors and all graduate.

"The architecture with any organization starts with the plat-form," Byrd said. "That was Elmer Love and Mike Wilhite. Then growth came with Ricky Free, myself, and Juan Mitchell. He had a recruiting class in 1975 as good as there was in the country, sans a big man. His strength was getting good players to come to school and stay in school. But he always had good players."

Before the turnaround, Penders' first team at Columbia was 4–22 overall and finished last in the Ivy League (2–12) in 1975. The next season the Lions doubled their victory total overall (8–17) and tied for fourth (6–8) in the league standings. Freshmen were not allowed to play on the varsity during Penders' tenure at Columbia.

"In my first two years at Columbia, I also learned that I had to change my style to compete with teams in the Ivy League," Penders said. "I learned to play at a much slower pace on both ends of the floor. I learned a Princeton-style offense and started to play various zone defenses. We had to do something to hang close to more tal-ented teams and shorten the games. I had to do this to survive. In my third year at Columbia, we played some up-tempo games against teams that we were better than. But we also played many games at a slower pace.

"We actually beat Princeton at Princeton, 38–36, my final season there (1977–78), which was one of the greatest wins of my career. We also blew out teams like Dartmouth, Cornell, and Harvard by pressing and running. I still strongly prefer an up-tempo style, but I really learned to adjust at Columbia. I might have ended up selling basketball shoes at age thirty if I hadn't."

Columbia turned the corner with Penders in 1976–77 when Byrd started at point guard as a sophomore and Free moved into the lineup as a scorer. Other top players were Juan Mitchell and Shane Cotner.

Early in the season, Columbia won 85–75 at Rutgers, which had been to the Final Four the previous season. "We led the entire game—no contest," Penders said. "After we won the game, I went in and told the Columbia athletic director Al Paul I wanted a new contract. And he balked and said, 'We will wait until the end of the year.' I said, 'I quit.' I took a big gamble. I thought Columbia will never be in this position again. 'You left me hanging last year. This is the final year of my contract. I am trying to recruit. If you are not going to renew me now, I am leaving and I will still be able to get a job.' Here I am twenty-nine or thirty years old and risking my whole career!"

Columbia was on its way to the Marshall Invitational in Huntington, West Virginia, when Penders received a call from Paul, who told him he had a new three-year contract waiting for Penders when he returned. Penders thanked Paul, but told him this would probably be the final contract that he would sign at Columbia, given the difficulties in getting it done.

In 1976–77, Columbia tied Seton Hall for the New York–New Jersey 7 Conference title. A group of seven major teams in the New York City–New Jersey area would schedule one game a week that would be televised in the area and would count toward a conference title. The other teams in the league: Mike Krzyzewski's Army team, Rutgers, St. John's, Princeton, and Manhattan.

Boston College made a pitch for Penders late in the 1976–77 season, but school officials in Boston wanted him to make a commitment before Columbia's season concluded. Lafayette's Tom Davis and Princeton's Pete Carril were the other coaches in the mix. "I was offered, but I said I had two weeks left," Penders said. "I said, 'I am not going to ruin my team's chances at Columbia.' We could have still won the Ivy League. Tom Davis took it because it was his best opportunity to get out of Lafayette. And I think Pete always saw himself as the Princeton coach."

Penders' third Columbia team finished the 1976–77 season with a 16–10 overall record and 8–6 in the Ivy League, good for third. Penders knew that might be the ceiling at Columbia. "But that was the first year we had won, and we had the whole team back and so I stayed another year," Penders said. "During that final season at Columbia, Alton Byrd suffered a sprained ankle and was out and we lost a few games that we would have won easily if he had been playing. Instead of winning nineteen or twenty games, we ended up winning fifteen. And I said, 'I am not going to depend on someone not getting a sprained ankle next year.' I moved crosstown to Fordham where I had scholarships to offer and where I didn't have to teach. I had to teach two quarters each year at Columbia. And my assistants had to teach during different parts of the year, too."

FORDHAM (EIGHT SEASONS: 1978-86)

Penders took his coaching style from Columbia to Fordham. His theme remained the same: Press and run if you were the better team, but play half court and mix up your defenses to keep your opponent off balance if you were short on talent. Keep turnovers to a minimum, always.

"When I moved to the Bronx and Fordham University in 1978, that was a different scenario in recruiting," Penders said. "The New York Catholic League steered their students to Fordham because it was a great school, and second- and third-generation families wanted their children, who were Catholic, to stay closer to home during that era. It was like how BYU and Utah have attracted the top Mormon students and student athletes over the years.

"Except for two Sudanese big men who landed in my lap, all of our players were from an eighty-mile radius of Fordham. Maybe two other players came from outside that area during my eight years at Fordham. The players came from working-class families, and none of them had Amateur Athletic Union coaches with their hands out or trying to act as agents. But unlike Columbia, kids aren't going to come from Overland, Ohio, to go to Fordham in the Bronx where they had ribbon-barbed wire around two-thirds of the campus. It was a tough area. It was in a high-crime area. You might hear fifteen to twenty gunshots on any given night."

One of those local New York finds for Penders was guard David Maxwell. "David was a real recruiting coup for me in my second year at Fordham," Penders said. "He was first team All-City and arguably the best player in the city. He played at Lew Alcindor's (later known as Kareem Abdul-Jabbar) old school Power Memorial. David didn't want to leave home. He was a great all-around player. Not a super shooter, but he could score and was an excellent defensive player. He patterned his game after Walt Frazier, the New York Knick who was still looked at as an icon in New York when David was growing up. David was defense first and super at stealing the ball one-on-one. I would always put David on the other team's point guard. Two or three times a game he would take the ball away and rattle the other team."

Just like Tufts and Columbia, Fordham had its challenges.

The Rams played basketball games in Rose Hill Gym, which was built in 1925 and was already more than fifty years old when Penders first arrived at the Jesuit school. Through the 2009–10 season, it was the oldest on-campus facility utilized by a Division I men's basketball program. Besides its various peculiarities, Rose Hill is famous for being the gym where Alcindor's Power Memorial High School team played his final high school game in 1965 before he went on to star at UCLA.

When Penders arrived in the spring of 1978, Fordham had no talent remotely comparable to Alcindor and had suffered through six straight losing seasons. Digger Phelps, later of Notre Dame coaching and ESPN analyst fame, had taken the Rams to the NCAA Tournament in 1971 and advanced to the Sweet 16. But that was Fordham's only NCAA Tournament appearance since 1954.

"There were newspaper stories about them possibly dropping basketball and going Division III," Penders said. "Their vice president called me on the 'QT,' and I accepted the job over dinner. It was my last year at Columbia in late February or early March. I would have fifteen full scholarships and a full-time staff. Nice dorm rooms. I knew I could win there."

At Fordham, Penders re-connected with Susie (Dubach), his future wife. He first met her at Columbia when she was a secretary in the Columbia football office. Then, when he got to Fordham, he ran into her at a party and the pair started dating in the spring of 1978. Susie, a Midwesterner from Illinois, graduated with honors from the College at Lincoln Center of Fordham University, receiving the prestigious Sophocles Papanicolaou Award for Outstanding Achievement in Art History and Studio Art. The Penders were married at the chapel on Fordham's campus in March 1980, and they stayed at Fordham for eight years largely because they liked the New York City lifestyle. Penders' name surfaced as a frontrunner for several coaching vacancies during that time, including one from Miami (Florida) to re-start its basketball program in the mid-1980s, but the Penders were very happy in New York. Penders established his reputation in the East as a solid coach of fundamentals. "I think one of Penders' greatest strengths is the way he teaches fundamentals," said Tony McIntosh, who played for Penders at Fordham. "He's helped me come a long way with my shooting. I have always had good mechanics. But I had to learn things like proper footwork and squaring up to the basket."

"When I came to Fordham, I was pretty much out of control," said guard Jerry Hobbie, another player for Penders at Fordham. "Coach Penders taught me how to run a ball club. We prided ourselves on making few turnovers."

Once again, Penders got the program rolling. After 7–22 and 11–17 seasons, he took the Rams to five straight National Invitation Tournaments during a time when the NIT was a big deal in college basketball. Penders also played an intersectional schedule that included such teams as Notre Dame, Syracuse, Arkansas, North Carolina, UCLA, Tennessee, Hawaii, New Mexico, and others, and really feared no team.

"I think one thing Tom did, he created an identity at Fordham," said Hobbie, a guard for the Rams from 1980 to 1985. "The five years I was there, we had a lot of success and we went to the NIT every year. We went after every team. We didn't back down. I think we took on Tom's personality. We maybe didn't have the facilities of some of the teams we were playing, but we had that kind of identity—a bunch of tough kids who fought for what we believed in. And that was a reflection of his personality.

"We had a bunch of throw-back guys and a core of about seven or eight guys who all believed the same way," Hobbie continued. "We were kind of like junkyard dogs. It didn't matter who we played—St. John's, North Carolina—we were going after them like we had nothing to lose. Some of the more highly recruited guys didn't play as much, because they were more finesse. They weren't as tough as some of the guys who got the minutes."

Rose Hill's environment matched the team's rugged attitude. The sun even became a factor during afternoon games because of the expansive windows at the top of the gym. It was like taking or not taking the wind in a football game.

"Sun was in your eyes at a certain part of the day on the court,"

Penders said. "Back in those days the visiting team could chose which basket it would take in the first half. You didn't have to take the basket going away from your bench. It was a gym where the sun came into play when we played a lot of Saturday afternoon basketball games.

"Teams would choose to take the west goal in the first half before the sun was really coming through there before it got low. In the second half it was coming right through the end-zone windows, right into the shooter's eyes. We practiced in there, and we were pretty used to it. A team that wasn't used to it, they would shoot 15 percent in the second half (if they chose the wrong end). Schools who played us all the time were wise to it."

During the 1980–81 season, NBC televised the Fordham–St. John's game at Rose Hill, but Fordham had to rent and install baseball lights because the gym was too dark for television. Even on sunny day games, the networks needed lights because of shadows left on the floor from the sun shining through the beams that supported the roof. The roof was also leaky and had holes in it. Birds, mostly grackles, would get into the building and nest in crooks and crannies near the roof.

"We would try to kill them, poison them, shoot them with BB guns," Penders said. "We had an equipment manager who would come out right before practice and the guys would have to stand in the corner for fifteen minutes while he was trying to kill these birds. Like New York people, New York birds were tough; they were tough to kill. I will never forget during the middle of one game: There was a big crowd there, and we may have been playing Iona. My assistant Jerry Houston had a clipboard with a big bird dropping on it the size of a softball. There would be droppings from nests. In practice, we would station a naïve assistant under the nest, and inevitably he would get a dropping on his shirt. That was part of the charm of Rose Hill Gym."

"I remember one game when I was shooting a free throw and I got hit by pigeon crap on my shoulder during the game," Hobbie said. "I had the ball when it hit me and I stopped. And I gave the ball back to the ref and the manager came out and wiped it off my shoulder. I told the ref, 'I can't miss now. It is good luck, right?' He started laughing. I made it."

Because of the smallish size and conditions at Rose Hill, Penders pumped up his schedule by playing selected big games at Madison Square Garden and then the Meadowlands.

"Frank McGuire had retired from coaching at South Carolina and Sonny Werblin, who made Joe Namath with the Jets, had become the director of Madison Square Garden. And he had hired his friend Frank McGuire to run college basketball there," Penders recalled. "Frank made every effort to keep college basketball near the top, although the Knicks always would be number one. We played North Carolina and Notre Dame at the Garden. He was helping me out. The Meadowlands Arena then came into the picture and we played one game a year there, like Syracuse or Notre Dame."

Penders' team in the Bronx that came the closest to making the NCAA Tournament was the 1982–83 team, which won the Metro Atlantic Athletic Conference Tournament with a 54–53 victory over Iona in the title game at the New Jersey Meadowlands. But the newly formed league did not have an automatic berth to the NCAA Tournament. Penders sat in the NBC studios in Manhattan to be interviewed by Bill Macatee, but a Selection Sunday full of upsets in tournament title games clogged the pool of potential NCAA at-large teams and the Rams were passed by and went to the NIT.

Another strong club was the 1984–85 team, which became Penders' fifth and last NIT team at Fordham. The ceiling had been hit. Under Penders, the Rams were 0–5 in NIT first-round games, but, alas, because of Rose Hill, all those NIT games were on the road.

"I wish Joe (Paterno, a star freshman in 1985–86) had been there my senior year the year before," said Hobbie, who had a fifteen-assist, seven-steal game against LaSalle that season. "We were one guy short, undermanned. We had three senior starters. I remember we lost at St. John's (47–46), which went to the Final Four."

By the start of the 1985–86 season, those seniors were all gone. Penders had a new athletic director, Frank McLaughlin, who had illusions of returning Fordham to football glory.

"At his press conference, the athletic director asked me to come and show support and I said, 'Sure,'" Penders said. "Then he gets up there and gets very emotional and teary-eyed and said his goal was to bring back Fordham football. He wanted to bring back the Vince Lombardi days. Football had one little locker room, an equipment room, one whirlpool, and no money. And we are taking vans to 90 percent of our games. I drove one of the vans. They went to I-AA (now Division I Championship subdivision). So all the money went into football.

"He and the school's president had a vision of Fordham going into a conference (the Patriot League) with Colgate, Bucknell, Lehigh, and Lafayette. No scholarships would be given in football and basketball. Holy Cross was going to join them. They were academic elitists. They were going to recruit nationally. I knew right then I was out of there. I still had four years left on my contract when he came on. I stayed one more year."

Penders left Fordham after the 1985–86 season, and the Rams have had only five winning men's basketball seasons since, entering 2010–11.

"When I left Fordham to go to Rhode Island in October of 1986, I took a pay cut of $10,000 because I felt that I would die a slow death at Fordham and Rhode Island had much better potential to win in the Atlantic 10 than Fordham did in the little Metro

Atlantic Athletic Conference," Penders said. "Rhode Island was in a league that was on television and put two or three teams in the NCAA Tournament every year. Temple was the number one team in the country for most of 1987–88. West Virginia and Penn State were strong, and so were schools like St. Joseph's and Rutgers."

RHODE ISLAND (TWO SEASONS, 1986-88)

Penders didn't get the Rhode Island job until right before fall practice started in the 1986–87 season. The previous coach, Brendan Malone, was on the final year of his contract and had re-signed early in September when Hubbie Brown hired him to be an assistant coach for the New York Knicks.

Penders knew Rhode Island football coach Bob Griffin, who was from Milford, Connecticut, near Stratford, Penders' boyhood town. Penders called and left him a message that he would be interested in the job. Eventually, Rhode Island athletic director John Chuckran called back. And Penders also talked to a couple of big boosters before meeting the full search committee.

"I may never have left Fordham if this didn't happen," Penders said. "There were thirty people in the room when I interviewed and about a dozen were my age who hated my guts (remembering him from his playing days at Connecticut). But they all ended up being very good friends of mine.

"Rhode Island had some good players and they were in the Atlantic 10, a higher level league. Billy Reynolds, a friend of mine and the columnist for the *Providence Journal*, said, 'This team is made for you. You can install that running game here.'"

The fans would buy it in Kingston because there was a tradition of running teams at Rhode Island. Frank Keaney, the Rhode Island coach from 1920 to 1948, introduced the "Runnin' Rams," which were usually among the nation's top scoring teams averaging in the seventies at a time when most teams scored in the forties and fifties.

Timing was everything for Penders in this job. Although the Rams had suffered through five straight losing seasons and had won only forty-two games over that period, they had the returning personnel to run and the college game was changing.

"When he first got there I liked what I heard, like he was sort of a players' coach. I liked the sound of that because we would have a little more freedom than the previous coach," Carlton "Silk" Owens said. "He came in with a positive attitude. He uplifted the team's spirit and that of the fans. He welcomed the fans into practice. And we had a family atmosphere we didn't experience the first two years."

In 1985–86, the 45-second clock was instituted, and when Penders went to Rhode Island in the fall of 1986, college basketball was adding the three-point shot. Interestingly, the first time the three-point shot was experimented with in college basketball was in a game between Columbia and Fordham back in 1945, two of Penders' schools.

"I think Rhode Island took nine three pointers all year under Brendan Malone," Penders said of the previous season when the Atlantic 10 was experimenting with the line. "My first team at Rhode Island, I think we took nine threes in the first five minutes. We took full advantage of it in 1986–87 and went 20–10 and to the NIT. It was too easy, and all of the young players immediately started practicing the three."

During Penders' first season, Pitino and Providence of the Big East advanced to the 1987 Final Four by raining three pointers, led by guard Billy Donovan. Then it was Rhode Island's turn to make a splash in the 1988 Tournament when they advanced to the Sweet 16.

"I was a pretty decent three-point shooter as well as Tommy Garrick," Owens said. "If we were open he would say, 'Take the shot.' That helped with building confidence. And that would open up the inside for those other guys."

"In 1987–88, Silk Owens and Tommy Garrick were outstanding three-point shooters," Penders said. "But we used the three to keep the defense honest. Owens and Garrick could also attack the rim and pull up at mid range. Six-foot-nine Kenny Green had a strong inside game and six-foot-ten Bonzie Colson was pretty good inside as well. Our other top players were six-foot-four John Evans and six-foot-seven Mergin Sina. Evans loved to drive, and Sina loved to pull up from fifteen feet. Both were aggressive offensive rebounders.

"We weren't deep beyond six players, but we were smart and balanced and had close to two hundred less turnovers than our opponents. We used the three-pointer to spread the floor and then we attacked the belly of the defense. We were fundamentally one of the best teams in the country and we never beat ourselves."

Penders recruited regionally in his two seasons at Rhode Island, which was running its basketball program on a shoestring budget. Penders had the lowest paid staff and salary in the league.

"My athletic director at Rhode Island, John Chuckran, had been a line coach for Joe Paterno at Penn State for more than twenty years. . . . He knew I had to move on after two years. I was the lowest salaried coach in the Atlantic 10. Our president at Rhode Island was embarrassed by our success. Rutgers had asked for permission to talk with me before I left for the Final Four. Rhode Island president Ted Eddy made a statement to the media, 'We thank Tom Penders for all that he has accomplished here, but I can't justify paying a coach more than we pay an English professor.' Despite the fact that I really loved John Chuckran, I knew I was as good as gone."

Rutgers approached Penders, but he put the Scarlet Knights

on hold when Texas called and interviewed him in Kansas City, Missouri, during the Final Four. The Longhorns talked big money at the time, a $400,000 package, eight times what Penders was making at Rhode Island ($50,000). Penders took the Texas job shortly after the 1988 NCAA title game.

PENDERS' NCAA TOURNAMENT RUNS

"The main thing I took from Penders as a coach was his positive attitude. He would criticize you, but in a good way. He is a positive person in life, which is something I took with me."
—Carlton Owens, Rhode Island guard

Tom Penders was usually the underdog in the NCAA Tournament while taking vagabond teams to the Big Dance. In eleven combined NCAA Tournament appearances at Rhode Island, Texas, George Washington, and Houston, his team was the higher-seeded in first-round games only three times.

"I called people who had tournament experience," Penders said. "One was Mike Krzyzewski at Duke (four NCAA titles: 1991, 1992, 2001, 2010) and the other was Al McGuire, who had been at Marquette and won the 1977 NCAA title. I was able to have dialogue with them on how to get my team mentally ready and in the right frame of mind.

"The biggest thing Mike and Al told me, 'You've got to be loose and you have to be confident no matter who you are playing. You have to find one or two things you feel if your team does well, you are going to win the game and sell it to your team.'"

RHODE ISLAND'S BIG RUN

In October 1986, Penders loosened up the Rhode Island program in a hurry. Jim Christian, a reserve guard, remembers a Penders speech that would help propel Rhode Island to a 28–7 record in 1987–88, the school's best mark at that time in eighty years of basketball. "He came in and took over our team two days before the start of practice," Christian recalled. "His first meeting with our team—and I will never forget it—because my friends and I still talk about it. We were not very good the year before when we had won nine games (9–19). The first thing he said: 'I have been around East Coast basketball for twenty years, and I don't know any of you guys.' Meaning we must not be very good. That same group of people two years later was in the Sweet 16."

Penders took the Rams to the NCAA Tournament in 1988 during his second year at the school. In 1986–87 at Rhode Island, Penders had a decent 20–10 record when the Rams went to the National Invitation Tournament.

"When we first came here none of us knew how to lose," Bonzie Colson, who played for a highly successful Dunbar Washington High School program told the *Providence Journal*. "That first year (with previous coach Brendan Malone) I actually sat down and cried after we lost. I'm not a quitter. . . . With Coach Penders it has been like a reincarnation."

Penders' first season at Rhode Island was all about changing the losing attitude and winning the close games. "And we lost a few games that first year we shouldn't have," Penders recalled. One was a 96–92 defeat to Final Four–bound Providence coached by Rick Pitino. But that loss showed Penders' some potential in his players.

In 1986–87, the Rams were missing a six-foot-seven forward transfer from Seton Hall, Mergin Sina, who sat out the first year. The Albanian, who was brought up and raised in Brooklyn, was an All-City player. He had the mentality of a point guard, played good defense, could shoot the three pointer, and averaged 6.5 rebounds a game in 1987–88.

Add Sina to a team with the dynamic backcourt of Tom Garrick and Carlton "Silk" Owens and the 1987–88 Rhode Island team was primed to do some damage.

"Nothing against the teams I had at Texas, but that was the best team, looking back, the soundest team," Penders said. "We only had seven guys who played, but that was a team that could have won the whole thing. We didn't turn the ball over a lot. We shot a high percentage. We had great inside players—Kenny Green, Bonzie Colson, and John Evans—and tremendous perimeter players who could also attack the basket and they were smart because of Garrick's (from Warwick, Rhode Island) and Owens' (Abraham Lincoln High School, Brooklyn) leadership."

Garrick and Owens each averaged more than twenty points a game and were close to 50 percent shooters. Garrick shot 55 percent from three-point range. The Rams committed about two hundred fewer turnovers than their opponents during the entire season and posted a 26–6 regular-season record with three of the losses to Temple, which wound up as the number-one-ranked team in the country.

Penders said Rhode Island was still sweating out getting an at-large bid after finishing second to Temple in the Atlantic 10 Conference tournament final. Rhode Island benefited from having West Virginia athletic director Fred Schaus on the Division I Men's Basketball Committee, which selects the at-large teams and seeds, and brackets the field. At the time, West Virginia was a fellow Atlantic 10 school.

"He was a class guy," Penders said. "Somebody on the committee who knew me told me that Fred Schaus stood up in front of the committee before he had to leave the room because they were talking about teams from our league. He said, 'If Rhode Island doesn't get in, then I am resigning.' We ended up getting in with a number eleven seed."

Number-six-seeded Missouri from the Big Eight Conference was the Rams' first-round opponent in the East Regional at the Dean Dome in Chapel Hill, North Carolina. Coach Norm Stewart of the Tigers had very little information on the Rams. And Stewart's Tigers were in a dangerous spot again. The previous season, fourth-seeded Missouri had lost to thirteenth-seed Xavier, Ohio, in the first round.

The Rams' tournament run, however, almost got short-circuited before it even began. The Rhode Island vans, which had been provided by the NCAA, got off track traveling to the game. For a 12:20 p.m. start, the team barely got there at 11:45 a.m. The vans left two and a half hours before the scheduled start of the game from the team hotel in what was supposed to be a twenty-minute trip. Instead, it turned into nearly a two-hour marathon through the wooded hills of North Carolina.

It had taken so long that Owens was asleep in the back of the van. Everybody jumped out when the van pulled up right in front of the Dean Dome. Police told the drivers of the team party, "You can't park there." But the vans were left unattended as the Rams hurried into the arena.

"I was worried about our team being flat," Penders said. "Silk Owens is a night owl. His first class was like at 11 o'clock. And Kenny Green was the same way. I was worried that we were not going to be ready for Missouri."

But Penders used the CBS analysis that Missouri and Syracuse would be a great second-round matchup to prime his team.

"Coach was great at getting guys excited and pumped up," Owens said. "He heard that Billy Packer said what a great matchup Missouri and Syracuse would be. He wrote 'Orange' on the blackboard. Let's prove them wrong. He would get me and Garrick fired up and that would filter over to other players. Once he got us fired up, we had the entire team and whole town behind us. He was a master at that."

Penders had put together his plan to win, convincing the team it could be done, in the words of Coach Krzyzewski or Coach McGuire. Forward Derrick Chievous, a New York City product, was the star of the Missouri team. Make life rough on him on the defensive end and shut down the rest of the team.

"Chievous was the main guy we were going to focus on—make it tough for him and exploit him as much as we could defensively," Penders said. "We had a good matchup with him trying to guard Garrick. He was supposed to be a really good defensive player, but Tommy was one of those kids who could hit the three, catch and shoot or shoot off the dribble, was a great penetrator, had a medium-range (shooting) game, and attacked the rim, too."

"And then we will zone them," Penders said. "They don't zone much in the Big Eight, and we hadn't zoned all year. They were not going to have any film of us playing any zone. And Mike suggested this. And we are going to meet Mike if we keep winning. He didn't have to say anything to me. But we were friends and still are."

Chievous wound up with thirty-five points, but he got in foul trouble trying to guard Garrick, who poured in twenty-nine with

Owens adding twenty-five. Nobody else on Missouri scored more than eleven points as upstart Rhode Island spurted ahead after trailing by two at halftime to post an 87–80 victory. With the score tied at fifty-six, the Rams scored nineteen of their final twenty-one points from the free-throw line as Garrick and Owens controlled the game.

"Norm tried some zone in the second half," Penders said. "And we were up by about eight points at that stage. We would eat up the 45-second clock, and with eight seconds to go we'd hit a three. We got three or four buckets that way, and that just took the wind out of Missouri. Our colors were North Carolina blue and white with some gold. And our fight song was the same tune as North Carolina's. Our band was there and playing our fight song. The North Carolina fans are thinking Rhode Island is happy to be in North Carolina and playing *our* fight song. So they got behind us in that game."

Rhode Island's second-round opponent was number-three-seeded Syracuse, which had lost the season before to Indiana on Keith Smart's baseline shot in the NCAA title game. The Orangemen were loaded with center Rony Seikaly, forward Derrick Coleman, and guard Sherman Douglas. But except for the 2,500 fans or so from Syracuse, everybody else was for Rhode Island. And the Rams, who had just won their first NCAA Tournament game in the first round, were heavy underdogs.

"We had started talking Syracuse as early as Tuesday to give them confidence, like, 'Hey we are going to beat Missouri!'" Penders said. "That permeates the team. 'The coach thinks we are going to win.' And then when you do win, you have some stuff in for Syracuse. Then you have one day of practice privately and focus on Syracuse. That was a great idea. I held on to that theory all the way through."

CBS had little respect for Penders' team. "Brent Musburger and Billy Packer were calling the game for CBS," Penders recalled. "They didn't come to our first game, and I don't remember them being at practice. They thought it was going to be Missouri–Syracuse. They came into my locker room about an hour before our Syracuse game and asked me to come down the hallway. And they ask me all kinds of questions about this and that and what do we do and how can we match up against Syracuse. Billy knew nothing about us.

"I told them that we match up really well with Syracuse, and they like to play zone. I said, 'We hadn't lost to a team all year that plays zone, other than Temple, and every time they played against us they came out in a zone and then played us man-to-man. We know how to attack zones. I am an Eastern coach. If you are an Eastern coach and you don't know how to attack a zone, you won't last two years in your job because Philly schools play zones and most of the teams in the East can play good zones.'"

The way to convince his team they could win: Shoot Syracuse out of their zone. They did. Wear them out with a press.

Rhode Island's Owens, Garrick, and Sina were great outside shooters and tore apart Syracuse's patented 2–3 zone in the opening twenty minutes. Rhode Island jumped to a fifteen-point lead in the first half and led by seven at halftime. Penders also used a three-quarters-court trap that frustrated and wore out the bigger Orangemen.

"Billy Packer kept saying Rhode Island has got to be tired, but Garrick was averaging thirty-seven minutes and Owens was averaging thirty-five a game," Penders said. "We were in great condition and those two could play all day. Kenny Green was our only inside guy, but we went right to him when they went to a man-to-man defense. Seikaly tried to play behind him and picked up four fouls. Coleman fouled out. And their backup center got in foul trouble."

Green scored twenty-three points, and Garrick and Owens combined for forty-six points.

There was a little talking back and forth between the two teams on the floor, but in the end Rhode Island had the last word. Said Owens to reporters after the game: "We were on a mission. We had to prove to the country that we were a great ballclub and the Atlantic 10 was a great conference. I think we proved that today."

"We were sweating to get in, now all of a sudden we are in the Sweet 16," Penders added. "For years I had the best record in the Dean Dome, 2–0, until my Texas team lost down there when we opened the 1994–95 season in a nationally televised game. It was a trivia question. I had a better record than Dean Smith there!"

In the Sweet 16 at the Meadowlands, Penders came face-to-face with Krzyzewski, fellow point guard whom he had scrimmaged against in college. They also coached against each other when Penders was at Columbia and Fordham and Krzyzewski was at Army.

Penders made the key call in this game when his star guard Garrick had three fouls with only seven minutes gone in the first half. That showed his team he believed in Garrick and them, and they responded with a great run that got them back into the game.

Duke opened the game with a typical 18–5 burst to assert its dominance. And Garrick picked up two charges and a foul on the defensive end.

"I said, 'Guess what, Tommy? You are not coming out,'" Penders recalled. "'You are playing. I don't care if you foul out in the first half.

We are going to a matchup zone, and if Danny Ferry (Duke center) gets the ball, we were going to trap him.' They had Robert Brickey, Billy King, and Quin Snyder. They tried picking us up full court. Our Kenny Green laid a screen on Quin Snyder, who had to be carried off the floor, and they stopped pressing us. We gradually caught up and took the lead and led at halftime."

Rhode Island had its last lead at 55–54 with 10:33 to play. Ferry rebounded, hooked Green's arm, and pulled him down on top of him, and the referee blew his whistle. The two exchanged elbows. Green got up quickly, and the officials called an intentional foul on him. Ferry made two free throws, and Duke got the ball out of bounds and scored for a four-point possession that put them in command.

"Before the next season they have an officiating video that the coaches and referees have to watch every year," Penders said. "And this play is in it under the 'you can't let this situation happen.' You have to see the first part of the play. Ferry hooks our player, but the ref doesn't see it. Kenny jumps up. Ferry doesn't come at him. But they call Kenny for the intentional foul. Then at the end it is down to the wire."

Rhode Island trailed by four points in the closing seconds of the game. Owens dribbled down the court, pump faked, and the Duke defender jumped at him. Owens went up and nailed the three-point shot and got clobbered. No call. It was right in front of the official, Sonny Holmes.

"That was my last game at Rhode Island," Penders said. "The first SWC game the following season we play Arkansas at home, and Sonny's got that game. He is from Arkansas to boot. After the (Duke) game I said it was a shame that there were two referees and some imposter out there. I didn't know who the hell Sonny was or what conference he was from. I never thought he was terrible or out to get me, but Duke got a pretty good whistle edge there. They usually do.

THE TEXAS RUN IN 1990

In Penders' first season at Texas in 1988–89, the Longhorns broke a ten-year NCAA Tournament drought when they made it as an at-large entry and settled in as a number eleven seed. That was a familiar spot for Penders because Rhode Island was a number eleven seed the previous season. The Longhorns followed suit with an upset of sixth-seeded Georgia Tech, 76–70, in the first round before losing to number-three seed Missouri, 108–89, in the second round.

Texas had the potent B-M-W three-guard machine of Lance Blanks, Travis Mays, and Joey Wright returning in 1989–90. And Penders added his first big recruits from the junior college ranks—six-foot-seven forward Locksley Collie and six-foot-eight Guillermo Myers from Lon Morris College.

"They didn't do a whole lot for us until February," Penders said of the two transfers. "They were in shape and we pressed. They were role players, great rebounders, and Locksley had a nice scoring touch in and around the lane, and a fifteen-foot jumper, jump hook, and some up-and-under-the-basket moves. Panama (Myers) could only do a jump hook, rebound, and block shots. He didn't care if he scored. And he was the perfect complement for Blanks, Mays, and Wright. We had Courtney Jeans (another guard) coming off the bench."

In addition, Penders also had two other newcomers off the bench—six-foot-eight forward Hank Dudek, a transfer from Richmond, and six-foot-five swingman Benford Williams, who was a Prop 48 and didn't play in 1988–89. Dudek was a good defender who could run the floor and didn't care if he scored. Williams was an athletic scorer.

"We didn't have a great inside game," Penders said. "So we had to rely on Travis driving or Joey or Lance. That was not my best team by far, but they went the farthest (in the NCAA Tournament).

They were tough street fighters with lots of confidence that some described as arrogance."

With the Southwest Conference getting its usual lack of respect in the 1990 NCAA Tournament, Texas was a number ten seed going up against number seven Georgia in the first round in Indianapolis.

"I liked our chances in both of those games, except we had to (probably) play Purdue at the Hoosier Dome," Penders said of potential second-round matchup against the number-two-seeded Boilermakers. "What happened is some Indiana fans went there and rooted for us. But we were outnumbered by 20,000 Purdue fans. We might have had 250 tickets that Texas fans bought."

Selling his team on winning the Georgia game was this: Wear a bigger Georgia down with the press. Penders then spread the floor in the second half and allowed the Texas sharpshooters to go one-on-one against Georgia's slower defenders.

Georgia led 41–40 at halftime, but the pace was still too fast for the Bulldogs. And then Texas turned up the pressure and pace even more and let Travis Mays go in the second half. Mays scored a career-high forty-four points and made twenty-three of twenty-seven free throws. Blanks added twenty-one points and Wright had twelve. No other Longhorn was in double figures in UT's 100–88 victory despite thirty-three points by Georgia center Alec Kessler.

"You're dealing with a great player in Mays, and we don't have anybody who can guard him," said Georgia coach Hugh Durham after the game. "You have to take into consideration that he's in a lineup with other excellent players. We'd double team (Mays)—get it out of his hands. Then they'd get it back in his hands."

Mays became Texas' all-time leading scorer at that point with his outburst against Georgia. "There was no doubt in every tournament appearance we felt we still had to prove ourselves," Mays said. "Georgia was looked upon as a power team. Kessler was an All-American and Green was a juggernaut of a guard. Bring it on. For me, I wasn't sure we were going to win. I wanted to set the record. I wanted to win so bad, if I didn't get the record, I would have another game to get the record. It was the journey, the challenge to prove ourselves and get a win.

"All our guys competed so hard in practice, we felt like games were easy. The games were gravy. Me getting forty-four, I was focused so hard individually there wasn't any pressure of the tournament. I thought there was no way I wasn't going to take this opportunity. I couldn't see tomorrow."

In the NCAA Tournament second round, Purdue offered the Longhorns a challenge of playing a good team before its huge throng of fans. But Texas was still probably a quicker team than the more methodical Boilermakers from the Big Ten Conference. Playing at the Hoosier Dome before thousands of Purdue fans was a motivational tool for Penders.

"Tom Penders motivated every time we played on an opponent's court," Mays said. "He told us, 'We will make this our gym . . . it is their gym, they say it is. But we will go out there and take over the gym.' He would always say how we are going to win on the road. They may say it is not our gym. But when we get between the lines, we will take over the gym."

How else did Penders sell his team on this win? This was probably won by a pep talk in the second half and also by Penders' strategy on the last play of the game.

Texas trailed by nine points with 12:43 remaining when, as Penders explained, he asked his players, "'Are they doing this to us or are we doing this to ourselves?' They couldn't guard us. I thought our offensive aggressiveness in the last few minutes had a lot to do with us winning."

After the timeout, the Longhorns settled down and won by a point despite scoring a season-low-tying seventy-three points. Mays made two free throws with seven seconds remaining to give UT a 73–72 lead. Then, after a Purdue timeout, the Boilermakers put the ball in the hands of Tony Jones who dashed all the way down the court and had a shot with one second remaining blocked by Myers, his fourth block of the game.

"It was a gamble," Myers said afterward. "I got lucky that he went up sideways because I was really worried about fouling him. When he got by our man (guard Courtney Jeans), I had to gamble. When I saw the intensity he had, I knew he was going to take it all the way. Then I was just trying to tip it away."

"I never put a guy on the ball because that guy (inbounding) is totally out of the play," Penders said. "I would rather have a guy stand back ten feet. I would rather play five against four. Why play four on four when you can play four on five? I will often go to a five-man zone and react to the ball and put my best athletes in the middle of the floor."

After UT's upset of Purdue, Penders personally went out to scout the Xavier (Ohio)-Georgetown game at the Indiana Hoosier Dome. Texas would play the winner in the region semifinals. "I looked at

Georgetown and thought they are going to play our game better than us because they are bigger and they are aggressive," Penders said. "I wanted no part of Georgetown. Pete Gillen (Xavier coach) coached a beautiful game. He ran when he had an opportunity and when he didn't he used the clock and spread them out. I remember Georgetown coach John Thompson was really upset after the game and said it was inevitable his team would lose after watching Texas play two games. There was no way, he said, we would have gotten by Texas. I said, 'Thanks for the compliment, coach.' But our kids were going to have a fear of Georgetown—the big bad Hoyas."

The Longhorns caught a break in the Sweet 16 because they were playing in the friendly confines of Dallas's Reunion Arena, where they had played only two weeks previous in the SWC Post-Season Tournament. But initially the familiar surroundings did little to help the Longhorns, who had a miserable first half and trailed the Xavier Musketeers.

"We refused to lose," Mays said. "We had something to prove. One bad half of basketball didn't bother us. We knew we had guns, and they would be unloaded when we were done. Lance (Blanks) showed so much in the second half."

Penders' eventual plan to win revolved around having a private
halftime chat with one of his star guards, Blanks, who had been
involved in an incident in a game earlier in the season against Texas
Tech. Red Raider coach Gerald Myers had accused Blanks of spitting
at one of his players. But Blanks claimed he was merely removing his
mouth guard and some slobber came out. Blanks had been quoted as
saying, "Who is Gerald Myers?"

"I think our kids were a little over confident against Xavier,"
Penders said. "We were down twelve at halftime (53–41), and Lance
had only two points. I didn't holler or get on them in the locker
room at halftime. I just said, 'This has been a great year.' There were
like ten minutes left in the halftime, and the other players went back
out. I said, 'Lance, come on back.' And I told him: 'You know what?
Gerald Myers is probably back in his living room popping a Pearl
Light Beer and smiling and saying, "I told you he was a punk."' Lance
goes out and scores twenty-six points in the second half. . . . We win
102–89, and we scored sixty-one points in the second half."

Blanks added, "I will tell you Coach Penders had the right words
at the right time. He was an inspiration. He always knew what buttons to push to get the most out of me. He had us believing we were
the best in the country at something at some point. He was really
good in those situations. . . . He would put you in the right frame
of mind to play the best that you could, and in some cases over-
achieve."

Arkansas easily beat North Carolina, 96–73, in the other semifinal in Dallas, setting up a SWC Texas–Arkansas matchup in the
regional final to go to the Final Four in Denver. The last time the
two teams played Arkansas had won 103–96 in overtime in Austin
when Razorback coach Nolan Richardson had strolled off the floor

without receiving a technical foul late in the game.

"We said we are going to get Arkansas this time," Penders said. "It's not going to be all Arkansas fans this time. They bought up all the tickets to the conference tournament (SWC). But they couldn't possibly have more than half of the building."

Texas wound up losing to Arkansas, 88–85, in a thrilling ending. The Longhorns came back from eleven points down with 7:30 remaining to within three points and had the ball with a chance to tie the score with less than twenty seconds remaining. Mays missed a three-point shot, just short.

"You are just bringing back pain, straight to my heart," Mays said. "They (Arkansas) were the team we couldn't match up with. Maybe with their first five we could, but they had a really, really deep athletic team and didn't want to lose to the University of Texas.

"I thought it (the three pointer) was down. . . . I fouled out after the miss and was just laying on the floor. I knew it was the last shot I would take in a Texas uniform. Some people thought I was hurt. Tom came out on the court. Knowing it was the end, he said, 'Just lay here for a minute. I know how you feel.' He had a complete understanding of where I was. We wanted to go to the Final Four so badly. The game was completely over, but my body was reacting like there was another game. After the game, Arkansas center Oliver Miller holding the Horns sign down. I will never forget it. But we lost to a very good team."

"It was a cruel twist of fate," said Blanks, now the general manager of the Phoenix Suns and still in close contact with Penders. "It was the same shot that Lee Mayberry made in an earlier game against us that season to send a game into overtime that Arkansas won. It was a mountain we couldn't get over. I certainly felt it (the shot) has got to go in. What a disappointment. Even while we are talking about it, I can feel some disappointment and emotions. I remember that shot like it was yesterday."

Arkansas coach Nolan Richardson beat Texas for the third time during the 1989–90 season, but he said Coach Penders had done a "phenomenal job at Texas in his two years, taking them to the Final 32 and the Final 8."

"The University of Texas is the best basketball team we've played this year," Richardson said after the game. "And that includes all the teams in the tournament so far. There's no question in my mind if Texas was in the other bracket we would probably be meeting in Denver (in the Final Four). . . . It's very difficult to continue to beat a team as good as they are. Unfortunately, we had to meet in the regional finals."

PENDERS' GENERAL NCAA TOURNAMENT AXIOMS

For Favored Teams: "Psychologically, if you are the better team you have to put all your focus on the first game because all the pressure is on the favored team. It may not mean you are going to lose if you are a one or two seed because you are playing a fifteen or a sixteen seed. But if you are a five seed playing a Creighton at number twelve, you better have your team totally focused. You don't even mention the second-round opponent. You look at it as a one-game tournament. When you are a ten seed or higher, you talk about two games to build the players' confidence."

NCAA Practices: "When you have your first practice, the one-hour practice, you need to do half-court shooting games, free-throw shooting games, and jump shooting games. Have your worst defender try to guard your best ball handler. You need to keep your team loose. When that is over, take them over to a high school gym and have your real practice behind closed doors.

No Respect Card: "I remember when I was at Texas, we drew Oregon in the 1995 NCAA Tournament. Oregon was a very good team. And we were an eleven seed as the Southwest Conference champions. Even before they had the selection show, my athletic director DeLoss Dodds had called us and told us who we were going to play and where we were going. I told the team we had to build up our opponent, 'Oh, we don't have a chance, Oregon is so good. We don't get any respect. We have to be the hungry team.' I still remember the statement of Roderick Anderson, a guard on that UT team: 'I feel like I came down on Christmas morning and there was nothing under the tree. We had to go out to Utah and play. And we drew Oregon. We get no respect. We are better than a number eleven seed.' It worked, and we blew them out (90–73)."

STORIES GALORE

"Tom was down to earth, and it was more like dealing with a friend than a coach. He would just sit and talk about basketball. . . . He made a lot of friends and embraced the whole process of the media. He knew what guys were looking for and was not just trying to get good coverage. He would say things of interest, not just clichés. He would say some poignant things and was analytical. If he wasn't a coach, you would still like to talk to him."

—Happy Fine, former member of the New York media corps

PLAYING THE MIND GAME

P enders became a master of motivation during his thirty-six years as a head basketball coach on the collegiate level. The one player he didn't have to motivate most of the time was Lance Blanks, the new general manager of the Phoenix Suns. Blanks could always get under opponents' skin when he was playing at Texas.

Blanks, then a senior, proudly wore a "Texas: A Team Everybody Loves to Hate" t-shirt near the end of the 1989–90 season when the Longhorns made the Elite Eight of the NCAA Tournament. As a player, Blanks was certainly hated by opponents and coaches. Texas Tech coach Gerald Myers publicly asked if Blanks should get "The Jerk of the Year Award."

Penders loved coaching Blanks because he never backed down and always came to play. "It (my style of play) was always distracting for opposing coaches and players, but the sole purpose was to win— not to be a bad sport, but to win," Blanks said.

A player at McCullough High School in Woodlands, Texas, the six-foot-four Blanks originally went to Virginia, but transferred back to UT, sat out a season, and became eligible during Penders' first season of 1988–89. He actually transferred to Texas while Bob Weltlich was the coach. It's hard to fathom how Blanks' style would have fit under Weltlich.

In the end, Blanks flourished in Penders' up-tempo system and was a major reason the Longhorns made such a quick turnaround into an NCAA Tournament team. He became a potent, and contro-versial, element in the B-M-W offense, which also included guards Travis Mays and Joey Wright. Lance Blanks was also a first-round draft pick for the Detroit Pistons in 1990.

"He (Lance Blanks) was the most flamboyant and arrogant play-er who ever played for me, and he was very intelligent," Penders said. "He often put us and his teammates in situations where we faced hostile arenas. . . . Baylor had fans in a lot of sections booing every time he touched the ball and were yelling insults at him. After the game, the media would run right to Lance, who was the most quotable player. I would never tell the players what to say. I would advise them, 'Don't say anything that is going to be bulletin board material.'"

Blanks basically said what he wanted and carried himself on the floor with a confidence that went beyond his years. When he fol-lowed through on his shots with his signature move, it appeared as if he was waving to the other team. Besides being a big talker on the court, he also was accused of spitting at a Texas Tech player by Coach Myers. Blanks denied it and pointed out Myers' credibility suffered because the Red Raiders were 0–16 in Southwest Conference play.

"Lance basically ignored that (bulletin board warning)," Penders said, "and would make statements such as, 'They can't guard me. Our backcourt is way better than their backcourt. We have the best backcourt in the country. If I don't beat you, Travis or Joey will.' That kind of thing. The players would respond to it in the right way. Lance put everybody out there. We had a lot to lose if we didn't win. But with that particular group of kids, it was an extremely motivating factor."

ATLANTIC 10 FUN AND GAMES

At the Atlantic 10 Conference Post-Season Tournament in 1988, Rhode Island players refused to talk to anyone. The team was irritated that guard Carlton Owens was not the Atlantic 10 Player of the Year, guard Tom Garrick was not picked for the league's first team, and forward Kenny Green received no recognition.

Penders also was upset that the two-seeded Rams had to play three games in three nights if they were going to win the Atlantic 10 Tournament title. The Mountaineers, as the three seed and a two-time loser to Rhode Island, would only have to play three games in four nights if they advanced to the championship game. Top-ranked Temple, with guard Mark Macon, was the top-seeded team.

As a form of protest, Penders chose to stay and practice in Pittsburgh before the tournament started later in the week in Morgantown, West Virginia. The "us against the world mentality was in play."

"We didn't go down to Morgantown early because there was nothing to do out there, and we had poor practice times," Penders said. "A reporter from West Virginia writes a column how we stiffed Morgantown and walked out. He also writes in the column we are staying at a Marriott in Pittsburgh. And I start getting phone calls in my room: 'Don't come to Morgantown. You better have protection.' I left the messages on there, and we called ahead to the state police. A cop from West Virginia heard the messages. So we have a police escort with our bus going to Morgantown and a cop standing right outside my room at the hotel."

Rhode Island overwhelmed Rutgers, 104–73, in the quarter-finals. West Virginia had already won its quarterfinal the previous evening and had a day's rest.

Because it was an Atlantic 10 Tournament game and not a West Virginia home game, Penders requested conference officials to cancel the usual West Virginia laser show before the game and prohibit the firing of the musket by the Mountaineer Mascot stationed near the Rhode Island bench. Penders made sure the Mountaineers also had to wear road uniforms because they were the lower-seeded team in the tournament.

"It was a blood battle," Penders said of a 65–63 Rhode Island victory that set up a Rams' title-game meeting against Temple, the Atlantic 10 Conference regular-season champion. "We were going to get no more than two teams from the A-10 into the NCAA Tournament. We had no shot unless we beat West Virginia. And we were going to have to beat them for a third time. Their fans were howling at us and throwing stuff at us. After we won and went back to the same hotel, John Chaney (Temple coach) and I were the only ones left. We were roaring. He hated going there as well. The next day the title game was on television and we played before a lot of empty seats. Temple won, 68–63. But the tickets were all paid for, so the tournament didn't lose any money."

THE AL MCGUIRE EFFECT

Tom Penders spent a lot of time with the late Al McGuire before and after McGuire won the NCAA title in 1977 with Marquette. The colorful McGuire beat North Carolina and Dean Smith in Atlanta and then retired after the national title game. A much younger Penders always listened very carefully to McGuire, who said he retired because he was tired of dealing with bureaucrats (athletic directors) who could only communicate through memos. He said for coaches to survive they needed to have complete trust in their athletic director.

McGuire had several other theories about athletic directors, such as be careful of athletic directors who "say one thing to you and another to the media"; "an athletic director should never talk to an assistant unless he tells the coach in advance or asks the head coach to be present; if the athletic director normally makes road trips and he suddenly stops, the coach has lost his support."

"Al didn't compile his incredible record because of his ability to break down film or come up with complicated strategies," Penders said. "He knew people and could spot a phony from a mile away. I paid attention to everything he had to say, and it had a lot to do with my success and longevity in this great game.

"He was a master recruiter who focused mainly on the New York metropolitan area. He didn't want Milwaukee (where Marquette is located) players on his team because he didn't want to deal with 'Little League Parents.' He knew New York City kids lived the game, and that they had to be tough to survive the streets and the hard knocks that they handed out in New York.

"He knew it was all about people and trust. The more you understood people the better you were prepared for the challenges life would bring. I miss Al McGuire."

DEFENDING AL SKINNER

Penders' former assistant coach at Rhode Island, Al Skinner, had a successful thirteen-year run at Boston College that ended in 2010. He had a 247–165 record in thirteen seasons and won more games than any coach in Boston College history. His teams won three Big East titles and made seven NCAA Tournament trips, advancing to the Sweet 16 in 2006.

But the Eagles posted only a 15–16 record in 2009–10 (6–10 in the ACC) and failed to go to post-season play. Gene DeFilippo is quoted in several articles blaming Skinner for poor attendance at the Conte Center. Wow, since when are coaches responsible for marketing and ticket sales? Playing in a professional sports town like Boston, BC basketball has always struggled to increase their fan base. Even when I played at UConn and Bob Cousy was their coach they couldn't draw flies despite a gaudy record. Hockey outdraws basketball at BC.

In an ESPN.com article (March 30, 2010), Andy Katz quotes DeFillippo, "We want a coach who is going to play a very exciting brand of basketball. We want a team that's going to dive for loose balls, that's going to take charges, that's going to play great defense, and a team that's going to give us everything they have to give while they're out on that floor."

There is not a tougher, smarter basketball guy in the country than Al Skinner as far as I am concerned. He is a hard-nosed, hard-working, dedicated guy. To even suggest that Al's teams didn't play exciting or tough enough and didn't play hard is absurd! It's better to say the guy stays out until two o'clock in the morning than to question the man's work ethic. Anybody from the ACC, the coaches, would tell you Al Skinner is one of the best coaches to ever coach in the conference.

"Al burns inside. There is fire in his belly. He always had it, but he never would show it on the outside. Every now and then you would see him blow up on a referee. Rarely did you ever see him blow up on a player. He believed like I believed: You never showed a player up. Never. If you had to deal with a player, you did it behind closed doors."

One of those occasions was during the 1987–88 season. Rhode Island was playing a January non-conference game at Ivy League Brown. The Rams trailed 56–44 at halftime against a poor Brown team and had played miserably. On the long, very long, walk to the locker room, Penders said, 'Al, this is your halftime. I am liable to break a window or say something that will get me fired.'"

Penders stood outside the locker room and heard the high-pitched voice of Skinner. "I hear this crash boom bang @$$$@%@. And the team comes charging out. And I asked, 'Al, what happened?' And before he could tell me, one of the players told me, 'Al just went ballistic.' He threw a garbage can and one of those rolling black-boards. I even think he kicked John Evans off the team for giving a wise-ass answer.

"John told me, 'Al said I should just go sit on the bus.' I said, 'Coach Skinner was absolutely right. But I am going to give you a chance. I am going to play you the first five minutes of the second half. I don't care if you score a basket, just draw some charges and dive on the floor. He was a role player, a six-foot-five forward who could not shoot from the outside. He came out and had an incredible second half, scoring nineteen points in the game, and we won going away. Al Skinner set the tone."

ON THE TOURNAMENT ROAD

Many of today's coaches are afraid to enter tournaments where there are good teams and neutral officials. A major team, such as Syracuse, rarely leaves home during the non-conference portion of its schedule.

"Over the years, I have taken my teams to at least thirty-five of these types of events for educational and financial reasons," Penders said. "All of your expenses are covered, so the school can play games away from home at no cost. Your players get to see another part of the country and even the world. Every tournament has events planned for the entire group that are often cultural and educational. A place such as Alaska offers an amazing experience for anyone. I remember on a trip there that a player saw snow for the first time. I have taken teams to Hawaii, Alaska, Belgium, France, Yugoslavia, Australia, Puerto Rico, Montana, Utah, and Florida to name a few.

"I have never regretted taking a team to a tournament and showing them somewhere that they have never been. I have formed many worthwhile friendships during these travels. And many of our players have gone back to, and even live in, some of these locations. Coaches who are reluctant to travel with their teams for fear of losing games are cheating their players out of extremely valuable educational opportunities. It's part of the persona of the modern-day college coach: 'Don't leave home unless you absolutely have to.' Today, there are so many coaches who build a phony résumé by beating up on the smallest, weakest, and lowest-budgeted programs. And then they move on with a glossy but padded won/loss record. Why athletic directors allow coaches to do this is totally beyond me."

Besides the aforementioned opportunities, there were plenty of unforgettable game-time episodes, both good and bad, and often humorous in nature.

Penders' 1981–82 Fordham team played in the four-team 1981 Lobo Classic at The Pitt in Albuquerque, New Mexico. In the opening-round game, Penn was leading Fordham at halftime, but neither team was playing particularly well.

The walls were thin between the two locker rooms. And the Fordham team could hear Penn Coach Bob Weinhauer chewing out his team for playing poorly. "I got in there to hear the end of it," Penders said. "He was talking about beating these guys by thirty. He was ripping us. I didn't have to say a word to my team. I said, 'Well, you heard what their coach said about you guys. If you want to prove him right go out and play as badly as you did in the first half. But I think we will be fine in the second half.' We were a great free-throw shooting team. And I said when we get ahead of them, we will put the game away."

Eventually, Fordham beat Penn 77–73 in double overtime. But the game was almost a sideshow to the chattering going on between Fordham guard Mark Murphy and Penn assistant Doug Collins, the four-time NBA All-Star and U.S. Olympian and later head coach in the NBA, television analyst, and current head coach of the Philadelphia 76ers.

"Mark Murphy was becoming irritated because Doug Collins was yelling and saying things to him all game and provoking him," Penders said. "Murphy was kind of a cocky, arrogant player. He was a six-foot-two tough Irish kid who could shoot the lights out, but he wasn't one of my better defensive players. I believe we were playing a matchup zone at the time. So, as soon as we took the lead, Murphy turned and glared at Collins and said something to him. Then there was a timeout when Collins was yelling at Murphy all the way off the floor. Then I heard Murphy say, 'Yeah, yeah, yeah, Doug, what happened in the '72 Olympics?'"

Murphy was an historian of the game. Collins was a part of the USA team that lost the controversial decision in the gold medal game to the Soviet Union in the 1972 Munich Olympics. Murphy had had enough of Collins and wanted to let him know he wasn't going to take it anymore.

After the game, the teams shook hands and Collins was scolding Murphy. He then approached Penders, who recounted their conversation: "Collins said, 'That Murphy guy is a wise guy. You need to get him under control.' I said, 'I need to get him under control? What about you? Where does an assistant coach get off yelling at an opposing player?' He didn't like that. And until this day, he remembers that. I thought Collins was way out of line doing what he did. A coach, particularly an assistant coach, should not talk to players on the other team. He was just trying to get into Murphy's head, and then Murphy shot back at him and embarrassed him."

LOSING TO THE NEW MEXICO TIMEKEEPER

The next night Fordham played tournament host New Mexico in the title game, and Penders did the only thing that he believed would allow the Rams to stay in the game with the more athletic Lobos. He controlled the tempo against Gary Colson's team. The New Mexico band would always play until the Lobos scored, with the students standing and cheering.

"We held the ball for two minutes then called a back-screen lob play to take the crowd out," Penders said. "Sure enough, it worked. We dunked it. I don't think they scored for six minutes. And the New Mexico band got so tired that they finally quit playing and sat down. It ends up going right to the wire."

With the score tied and less than five seconds remaining, New Mexico scored a basket to take a 51–49 lead. The Fordham captain called a timeout with two seconds remaining. But the Western Athletic Conference officials from New Mexico's league didn't recognize the Fordham timeout. "The referee had to see him call the timeout because it was right in front of him," Penders said. "The official looked straight at our player, then turned and ran up the tunnel. We never got a chance to tie the game. I actually got a trophy for being Mr. Congeniality for not complaining after the game. The media asked me if I thought there was time left, and I said the timer may have gotten caught up in the flow of the game."

DEAN SMITH'S GAMESMANSHIP

"Opening the 1994–95 season when I was at Texas, we were playing at second-ranked North Carolina in a nationally televised game," Penders remembers of North Carolina's 96–92 victory. "Rasheed Wallace, North Carolina's star forward, is throwing elbows all over the place. Our Reggie Freeman fouled North Carolina's Dante Calabria going in for a layup, and the ACC official called it a hard foul. I questioned it. Reggie reached over and got part of the ball. Calabria put on the act a little bit and rolled into the support. North Carolina coach Dean Smith was almost to half court and was looking at me as if to ask, 'What is going on here?' Out of respect to him, I didn't say anything back."

Later, Penders, after looking at the tape, sent Smith a note: "Coach, I know you are upset about that hard foul. But if I was a referee, I would not have called it an intentional foul. Reggie's not that kind of player." Smith sent Penders a note back saying, "It was in the heat of the battle. I understand."

LEARNING FROM BOB KNIGHT
AND WRITING FOR *SPORT MAGAZINE*

During the 1975–76 season, Penders' second year as a Division I head coach, Columbia dropped a 106–63 decision to the eventual NCAA and unbeaten national champion Indiana Hoosiers early in the season. The Columbia-Indiana game was in the first round of the eight-team Eastern College Athletic Conference Holiday Festival at Madison Square Garden.

Before that game Penders went on local New York City television and cracked: "They kept drawing and on the fourth drawing, Coach Knight drew us." The personable Penders drew the attention of Dick Schaap, editor for *SPORT Magazine*. The late Schaap commissioned Penders to write a story on what it was like for an Ivy League school such as Columbia to play the number one-ranked team in the country.

"Bob Knight spent his entire press conference after the game, talking about what a great job I was doing," Penders said. "I couldn't believe he was doing this. It made an impression on me that whenever I can help a coach who is building a program, I try to help the guy. He could have buried me. He could have said, 'I would like to play these guys nine more times.'"

That following summer, Penders spent time with Knight at his camp in Bloomington, Indiana, and in the fall went to the Hoosiers' practice for three or four days before Columbia's started. At Knight's invitation, Penders stayed at his home. After practice, Penders visited with Knight and his mentor, the late, great former California coach Pete Newell. "We stayed up until 3 in the morning talking basketball Xs and Os and how to get the ball into the post and how to defend the post and things that are still very much with me," Penders said.

"One night at Bob Knight's home, the legendary Pete Newell was lecturing on fundamentals. He had many points, such as, 'When you're defending a guy who is going to try to pass it into the post while he's still dribbling, just concentrate on making him pick up his dribble and then pressure the heck out of him. Until he brings his left hand up to the ball, he can't pass it.'

"On shooting, Pete had some things that I thought were really important about footwork and balance. I continued to meet Coach Newell when he was visiting New York and I soaked up everything he had to say. What a genius he was. He was a class guy who had a true passion for teaching. I really miss the man. Bob Knight always treated older, veteran coaches with tremendous kindness and respect. He revered such older, veteran coaches as Clair Bee, Nat Holman, and Ray Meyer. That's a credit to the most misunderstood coach in history."

BAYLOR'S ROWDY CROWD

During his coaching career at Texas, some of the most unwelcome receptions Penders and Texas received were at Baylor's Ferrell Center in Waco, Texas. Maybe it was a coincidence, but the dislike for Penders may have had something to do with the fact he won sixteen of the first eighteen games as a UT coach against the Bears.

During a 96–91 Texas victory in Waco on February 6, 1990, Tom's wife, Susie, was the subject of sexually explicit words shouted by Baylor students behind the Texas bench. Susie was seated elsewhere but was informed of the sexually charged language by media personnel and some of the Texas players after the game. "I felt like I had been sexually abused," Susie Penders said. "I know those are strong words. But I had never in my life heard any insults that sexually explicit involving my name."

Baylor officials publicly apologized to Texas and the Penders after the incident and moved students away from the visiting bench. Later, Susie was asked to write a column in *USA Today* about harassment, asking, "What parts do ugliness and hatred play in college sports? When you make fun of an individual or scream slurs, believe me, it is painful. There is no justification for such behavior."

The following season, another incident occurred in Waco when Texas registered a 100–95 victory. A fan behind the bench was escorted out of the Ferrell Center after heckling Penders. Several times police officers had to turn people away from the bench. When UT won, the players had taken so much abuse they taunted the pro-Baylor crowd.

"There are so many slurs thrown at you, at the end of the game and you are up, you are very emotional," Texas guard Joey Wright said. "The slurs were on the court, off the court, and under the court. At one point, the crowd was getting so riled up, the parents and the kids were sitting next to them uttering profanity."

MOTIVATION, PENDERS' STYLE

During Rhode Island's great run in 1987–88, Penders used one of his motivational ploys to get Tom Garrick mentally ready for a December game against Providence at the Providence Civic Center, a forty-five-minute bus ride from the Rhode Island campus.

"We told the team we were going to leave at 4:45," Penders recalled for the 7 p.m. game. "Then I had an assistant coach call each guy on the day of the game, except Tommy Garrick. I told them not to tell Tommy we are going to leave at 4:30. We told them we would take care of it. I was worried Tommy was going to be too jacked up for this game. So the whole team got to the bus except him at 4:25, and they were all excited to play."

Penders walked down from his office and boarded the bus at 4:30. Garrick arrived at 4:40 believing he was five minutes early. Penders told Garrick he was late and would accept no excuses. He told him to sit down in his seat on the bus.

"We get there and I said, 'Tommy I will let you start, even though you obviously were not ready for this game, because you showed up late.' He said, 'But, coach.' I said, 'Shut up, Tommy, obviously this game is not that important to you. Go out there and do the best you can. I am going to let you start because you are a senior.' Silk Owens was wise to what was going on. He had a snicker on his face. I think Kenny Green, did too. He was street smart. Garrick was just fuming. He had a look in his eyes like he wanted to kill somebody. But in the past he would get too jacked up and nervous."

With Garrick playing a super game, the Rams posted an easy 92–70 win over their biggest rival, Providence. "That night he was like a man possessed," Penders said. "Defensively, he took the ball away from Providence star Delray Brooks several times. Delray liked to bring the ball up and spin dribble, and Tommy would take the ball away, lay it up and in. As soon as the game was over, Tommy had figured it out, laughed, and said, 'I probably needed that.'"

PENDERS' CABBAGE PATCH KID

Fordham guard Jerry Hobbie, then a six-foot-two junior, became a legend during a game in the 1983 Stanford Invitational Tournament against top-ranked North Carolina. Nicknamed the "Cabbage Patch Kid," the lanky Hobbie from Elizabeth, New Jersey, stripped the ball from Michael Jordan in the opening minutes of Fordham's 73–56 loss to the top-ranked Tar Heels.

"I was not going to back down from him," said Hobbie, now a

first-year assistant coach at SMU. "We happened to be in a matchup zone, and I stole the ball on him. . . . They made it up bigger than it really was. The whole place was sold out to see North Carolina. They didn't know who Fordham was. So the Stanford fans got there to see North Carolina. And from that point on, the crowd cheered for everything I did."

Oddly enough, Hobbie made the Stanford all-tournament team and Jordan didn't after Hobbie scored twenty-one points in Fordham's 89–74 victory over San Jose State in the consolation game. Against San Jose State, Hobbie made thirteen straight free throws and drew chants of "M-V-P! M-V-P!"

"At halftime of the Stanford–North Carolina game, he was spotted and carried out by a group of thirty students," Penders recalled. "He was embarrassed. They dropped him at half court. There was a ball rack, and they ask him to shoot. And he banked one in from half court. They got the Stanford president to shake his hand. They even had a 'Hobbie Watch'—what he did in that game and every game the rest of the season was in their student newspaper. The students wanted him to transfer. They even offered to fly him out there for spring break."

THE GUY LEWIS SNUB

Tom Penders coached six seasons at Houston and has become obsessed with trying to get former UH coach Guy Lewis (1956–86) into the Naismith Basketball Hall of Fame in Springfield, Massachusetts. He believes there is bias towards Eastern coaches and a failure of Texas sportswriters to push publicly for Lewis's candidacy.

It's undeniable that Lewis had a tremendous impact on college basketball in ways that transcended Xs and Os. He greatly helped integrate basketball in the South with the introduction of African-

American athletes at UH. Lewis also worked behind the scenes to schedule the Houston–UCLA game in 1968 at the Astrodome. That game was the forerunner of the first Final Four in a domed stadium in 1971 in Houston. The game, which the Cougars won, 71–69, changed college basketball forever. *Sports Illustrated* labeled it as the "Game of the Century." Dick Enberg has called it the most significant sporting event that he ever worked.

"Texas sportswriters have never gotten together as a bloc to write that Guy V. deserves to get into the Hall of Fame," said Penders, who also became familiar with the Lewis legend when he was coach of Texas for ten seasons. "That's one of the reasons there are so many coaches and players from the Northeast in the Hall of Fame. Compare the record of Louie Carnesecca's (former St. John's coach) to Guy V. Lewis's record. There's no comparison. Louie won 527 games. Guy V. Lewis won 592 games. Carnesecca took St. John's to the Final Four once (1985). Guy V. took Houston to the Final Four five times (1967, 1968, 1982, 1983, 1984) and made the NCAA title game twice.

"I am not saying Lou Carnesecca does not deserve to be in the Hall of Fame. He probably does belong," Penders added. "The New York and Northeast media loved Carnesecca, and they all got together and supported his induction. But why is Guy V. Lewis not in the Hall of Fame?"

Penders believes old petty jealousies among the old Southwest Conference media have kept Lewis from getting the support necessary. Houston was a member of the SWC during the later years of Lewis's coaching career. "Everyone, sportswriters included, thinks the coaches who were winning in (the SWC) in the 1970s and 1980s were cheating. That's all I heard since I moved to Texas in 1988. And that's what people are saying in 2010. Guy V. Lewis's team never had an NCAA probation, but you can't convince sportswriters that went to other schools that he didn't break rules."

COAST-TO-COAST

RECRUITING

"I have won 648 games in my career that spanned four decades. I'd like to think that some of those victories were because of smart coaching. But 95 percent of the reason was because I was a smart and economic recruiter."

—Tom Penders

HIDING THE BIG MAN

Sonny Alvarado, a six-foot-seven forward, eventually became a pivotal player for the 1995–96 Texas team, which went to the NCAA Tournament. In March of 1996, Alvarado, then a senior, had the distinction of scoring the final points in a Southwest Conference–sanctioned game: a layup with 24.8 seconds remaining in UT's 75–73 loss to seventh-ranked Texas Tech in the final of the last SWC Post-Season Tournament.

Getting Alvarado in the fold, however, was a difficult process because Penders and assistant coach Vic Trilli had to make a trip to California to find out where Alvarado had been "kidnapped" the summer before his second year in junior college.

Texas got the recruiting bead on Alvarado in the spring of 1993 when his coach at New Mexico Junior College came up to Penders during an all-star game in Tyler, Texas, and told him he had a freshman named Sonny Alvarado, from California, who wanted to play at Texas. Penders started recruiting Alvarado and also found out that his uncle, Richard Alvarado, had attended UT and owned a department store in El Paso. Sonny appeared headed to UT after he played his first season in junior college.

"Sonny went home for the summer," Penders said. "And everything was fine until the end of the summer, and all of a sudden nobody knew where he was. His junior college coach called us and said he didn't come back. His mom said she didn't know where he was. He was like a missing person. What happened was he had worked at a camp and somebody convinced him to transfer and go to Gavilan College in the Garlic Valley up in northern California near San Jose."

Penders called the coach at Gavilan who finally admitted Alvarado still had an interest in Texas, where he had a scheduled visit. But Penders also found out Nevada–Reno and Arizona State were recruiting Alvarado. Penders flew out to California and met with Alvarado, who said he decided to attend Gavilan College because he had a daughter in the area.

"He said, 'I am not so sure (about this place). It's hard to even get a meal around here,'" Penders recalled. "They didn't have a dormitory. All these guys were living in some rental house and were living on microwave burgers and milk. They didn't give scholarships at junior colleges in California.

"Eventually, he and his uncle Richard came to Texas on the official visit. I think there were some deals going on behind the scenes with the other schools. I told Sonny if he took anything from the other schools, that was his business, but he wasn't getting anything to come to Texas. He wound up coming. I think he was happy, and we certainly were. I sometimes hope that Sonny took the money from the school that was trying to hide him in the garlic fields because he was a joy to coach and never asked me for a dime."

LANDING RICKY FREE

Penders' top New York City recruit at Columbia was six-foot-five Ricky Free from Boys and Girls High School in Brooklyn. Free, who had expressed an interest in attending an Ivy League school, was at the top of his senior class academically. Penders put on the full-court press to recruit Free.

"I'd go and watch him play at his high school and give a kid five dollars to watch my car during games to make sure the car was there when I got out," Penders said. "It was a tough, tough school. I went to every one of his high school games. His games were in the afternoon. And sometimes I would just let my assistants run practice. My first team at Columbia was so bad (4–22) that John Wooden probably would have quit coaching, and I didn't feel bad about leaving the team to my assistants to go watch this kid play."

As Free's prep career came to an end, he was a high school All-American and participated in the prestigious Dapper Dan Roundball Classic in Pittsburgh. The Kentucky Wildcats and Coach Joe B. Hall were hot on Free's trail as well as some other Ivy League schools and coaches.

Penders had watched Free play about twenty times back in New

York City, but the Kentucky coach had flown with five or six horse breeders in a private jet to attend Sonny Vaccaro's Dapper Dan Classic. Penders had practically blown his entire Columbia recruiting budget to fly to Pittsburgh and stay at the hotel where all of the players and coaches stayed.

"Ricky knew I was there," Penders said. "I had an assistant there and an alum from Pittsburgh who had me paged throughout the game, so the kid would know I was there. And all the other coaches were ticked off. I think he had me paged five times during the Dapper Dan game.

"Then, I met Ricky right after the game, while everybody else was waiting back at the hotel where the coaches and players were staying. I headed him off, brought him in a side door and up an escalator to the second-floor elevator up to his room and suggested that he go out for burgers or suggested his roommate do it. Then I hung out with Chuck Daly of Penn and Joe B. Hall down in the lobby and acted dumb.

"Ricky was a shy young man and extremely bright. He had narrowed his list of schools and eliminated competitors like St. John's, Rutgers, and maybe a hundred others. I had convinced him that the Ivy League was the best option for a straight-A student like him and he really didn't want to talk to other schools. Joe B. Hall might not have known all about this, but I would have told him if he asked. Hell, he didn't even know who I was."

Back in New York City after the Dapper Dan Classic, Penders still had to fend off Kentucky, which was putting together a team that would win the NCAA title in 1978. "Ricky's mother and I got to be really close by talking on the phone and visiting at the family's apartment," Penders said. "All of sudden she called me one day and said, 'Coach Penders, you've got to get over here right now. Kentucky keeps calling and coming to the door and Ricky's staying in his room.'

"I went over there—it was the Red Hook section of Brooklyn—and most of the kids on the street knew me as a coach in that area. They would also tell me some other coaches had been there and they were from Kentucky. I told them, 'Well, keep those coaches away from Ricky; don't let them talk to him.' So they told them that Ricky was out of town, and that he wanted to go to Columbia. It was kind of a team effort, getting help from the neighborhood. The Kentucky coaches were like fish out of water in terms of knowing their ways around Brooklyn and New York."

Free wound up going to Columbia and was a 1,000-point scorer (1,214 points) and holds Columbia records for season (59.8) and career (55.2) field goal percentage.

"We didn't win the Ivy League title (with Free), but we became one of the better programs in the East," Penders said. "Penn and Princeton were both regulars in the Top 25, and Penn actually made the Final Four in Ricky's senior year at Columbia. Ricky and I still maintain contact, and he went on to have a very successful career in advertising. He could have played professionally but the money was better on Park Avenue, and Ricky got his degree from Columbia in four years."

NEW YORK CITY TIES HELP BRING RENCHER, FREEMAN TO TEXAS

Penders used his background and knowledge of the New York City streets to help land two stars at Texas—Terrence Rencher from St. Raymond's High School in the Bronx and Reggie Freeman from Rice High School in Manhattan. Rencher came first and then Freeman, who also lived in the Bronx, followed.

These two New York City players helped give Texas basketball an attitude and work ethic in the 1990s that permeated the program.

Rencher became the all-time leading Texas scorer during his career from 1991–92 through 1994–95, surpassing Travis Mays' career scoring record. Rencher was the star in 1995 when Texas claimed the regular-season (tie) and post-season tournament titles. Freeman was two seasons behind and helped lead Texas to an NCAA Tournament Sweet 16 finish in 1997, his senior year.

"Terrence, a smooth lefty, was a total player as he stuffed the stat sheets with assists, steals, and a lack of turnovers," Penders said. "He was a quiet assassin who played with unbelievable control and poise. Reggie Freeman, another lefty, stood six foot seven and almost single-handedly led us to the Sweet 16 in 1997. The great Kevin Durant was unable to do that for Texas years later. Reggie was a phenomenal player on both ends of the floor who just got better by leaps and bounds every single year. Reggie could run all day and never get winded.

"Reggie and Terrence had great respect for the game and played twelve months a year, which was a great thing for our Texas kids to see because many of them were used to playing seven or eight months a year. Rencher and Freeman grew up playing in the Boys' Clubs with no air conditioning or on the blacktop in outdoor parks in the Bronx and Manhattan. As well as their obvious skills, they also were natural leaders who showed their teammates how hard they worked at their game. The others guys tagged along and developed some of the passion that they brought to the program. They weren't flashy players either like the stereotype that sometimes exists for New York City players. They respected the game, and they knew how to play the game with great efficiency."

Penders says Rencher, now an assistant men's basketball coach at

Texas State University, could have played for any team in the country. Rencher rarely turned the ball over, and by the end of a game he would have scored twenty quiet points. He held together a team of very good high school players and could play the point and direct the team.

"You would look at his stats and he was nine out of ten from the floor, eight out of ten from the foul line, no turnovers and six assists, and four steals," Penders said. "He just quietly and very efficiently played the game. There was never anything fancy in his game. He averaged only fourteen or fifteen points a game in high school, but he was first-team All-City because he played on a team with a lot of good players and was very unselfish."

Rencher was already at Texas when Penders went to see Freeman while a bevy of Eastern coaches were ogling his highly recruited Rice teammate Felipe Lopez, who would wind up at St. John's. Penders had decided to go to the school to watch a pickup game. "I got to his high school at 2:30 p.m. and they played at 3," Penders said. "Reggie was waiting outside for me. I would drive up in a limo. Whenever I recruited in New York City a former walk-on player of mine at Fordham, Tony Censullo, would have one of his limousines pick me up at the airport and cart me around to the high schools. Many of my old coaching friends in the East would stare in disbelief when they saw me climb out of a limo in Harlem or the South Bronx. Tony Censullo was, and still is, a very successful Wall Street broker and a great friend of mine.

"Reggie saw me, and he yelled at me, 'Hey, Coach P.!' He said, 'Coach you have to watch me. Felipe is going to stay in New York. I am the guy. And I love Terrence Rencher. He is my man. I want to go to Texas.' I said, 'All right, Reg, I will watch you.' He put on a show with ten steals. He couldn't shoot outside of ten feet, but he would be following every shot, tipping it in. Or, he would throw it off the backboard and go in and get it on the other side and make an up-and-under shot.

"For a kid his size, at that time he was a skinny six foot six, he could really handle and pass the ball. I liked what I saw. And I didn't have a home visit planned with him. But he chased me down and asked me if I could meet his mom. He lived right over by the Sheridan Expressway. The trucks were twenty feet from his window. Every time a truck drove by, the whole building shook. He had this little room with a regular bed. His feet hung over the bed. And his room was filled with these trophies from when he was a little kid. I got there at 5 o'clock and left at 10 o'clock. We got him down to Texas, and he didn't visit any other school."

LANDING A SEVEN FOOTER

One of Penders' most unusual recruits was the late seven-foot-tall Dud Tongal (pronounced Dude), discovered by way of the United Nations. The recruitment of Tongal actually started during Penders' last season at Columbia in the very first game of the season. Tongal actually played for Penders at Fordham the following season.

In the opening game of the 1977–78 season, Columbia beat City College of New York (CCNY), 95–66. It was a routine victory for Penders' Lions, but sitting in the crowd with a consulate for the Sudanese Mission was Tongal, who was watching his first game of American college basketball. Previously CCNY coach Floyd Layne had toured Africa with several NBA players, including local NBA star Tiny Archibald. Layne had hopes of landing Tongal.

"The next day I get a call from this gentleman who said he had his nephew with him at the game the night before, and the young man would be very interested in attending Columbia," Penders recalled. "I asked how tall he was and he told me seven feet. After the phone conversation ended, I realized that I didn't get his phone number. I was so excited about getting a seven-foot guy, I forgot to get his phone number! I was sitting there in utter disgust at myself, and about twenty minutes later the guy calls back and gives me his number."

The next night Penders met the consulate and his family at the consulate's apartment overlooking the East River. All the family members were there and some other Sudanese consulates. The shortest person there was six foot seven.

"Dud was there and was very polite," Penders said. "He didn't speak fluent English, but he understood it. He spoke Arabic, French, and another tribal language. He was a cousin of Manute Bol. He verbally committed to Columbia, but he had to improve his English before he could be admitted."

In the meantime, Penders got Tongal a job in a restaurant bar named Arthur's Court (this was legal under NCAA rules in those days). The sports celebrity hangout was owned by basketball legend Art Heyman, who had been an All-American at Duke and first-round draft pick of the New York Knicks. Art was a real character on and off the court and had more than bill collectors looking for him in 1978.

"Tongal worked in the kitchen," Penders said. "And then the next thing I know, Duke's recruiting the kid because that's where Art went to school, and he tells the Duke coach at the time, Bill Foster, all about Dud Tongal. Bill flew into New York City to meet with him. I was pretty upset with it. But Bill backed off from him. Then that spring I left Columbia to go to Fordham. And right away it becomes a big story: What is going to happen to Dud Tongal? He still hasn't enrolled at Columbia. Well, he comes out and says, 'I am going with Coach Penders. My interest is playing for him and I'm going to Fordham.' So he's the first guy we signed at Fordham."

Penders had to find adequate housing for his first signee. The dorm rooms at Fordham were small and the beds not large enough for Tongal's seven-foot frame.

"Finally, we found some off-campus housing," Penders said. "It was mainly graduate housing, but we got him a room on the top floor that overlooked the Bronx Zoo. And it kind of made him feel like he was home in Africa. He could see giraffes from his room."

Tongal would become an important piece of Penders' rebuilding process at Fordham. He blocked fifty-six shots during the 1981–82 season and graduated as the school's career blocks leader.

AUBREY COLEMAN: HOUSTON GEM

Penders' Houston Cougars ended up with one of the best players in the city before the 2008–09 season. Aubrey Coleman was not really a highly publicized player because of his circuitous route to the Cougars: He went to defunct Gulf Shores Academy in Houston and later Southwest Mississippi Community College.

"He would play with our kids in Hofheinz Pavilion at our camps in June," Penders said. "We have all of our players work in camps. I saw this kid could fly, and he was an unbelievable athlete. He wasn't a shooter, but he was a scorer and could get to the rim. He was an incredibly well-conditioned athlete. He later committed to us. He wanted to stay close to home because his mom was sick. He ended up being the best all-around player I ever had."

Because of a keloid, a non-malignant, non-contagious growth that sprang from his neck, Coleman didn't play much high school basketball. Houston's Gulf Shores Academy, which has produced such stars as forward Gerald Green and guard Wink Adams, finally gave him a chance.

"He's a kid who hardly played high school basketball," Penders said. "He didn't play until his senior year. Gulf Shores Academy allowed him to play. But he had no college scholarship offers. His grades and test scores were okay. He went to junior college. And some junior college people told us that he was not getting a lot of attention. He was a rebounder and six foot four and could really push the ball."

Part of the reason Coleman selected the Houston Cougars was to be close to his mother, who also suffers from keloids. The growths can be surgically removed, but often grow back larger than before. They can cause other serious health problems.

"He was the most unique player I have ever coached," Penders said. "He played with such intensity. He went after every loose ball, and he dove on the floor. When he came to us, he was not a very good shooter. He was like Reggie Freeman his freshman year at Texas. But he worked extremely hard and became a good shooter."

In his senior season, Coleman led NCAA Division I scoring and was a key player in Houston's Conference USA post-season tournament championship.

TOM PENDERS' RECRUITING RULES

"I have won 648 games in my career that spanned four decades," Penders said. "I'd like to think that some of those victories were because of smart coaching. But 95 percent of the reason was because I was a smart and economic recruiter."

Below are some things that I learned about recruiting over thirty-six years of college coaching. Remember that this is my list of recruiting beliefs. This worked for me, and I feel that it will serve anyone who wants to have a long and happy career. The story will be short and sad if you don't have a basic core of beliefs. I don't care what time you get to the office or how many hours or days that you spend on something. It's the quality of your work that counts.

1. Don't waste time recruiting players who are long shots for you and your school.

2. You need to be a great judge of potential and talent.

3. Know as much as you can about the character of a prospect.

4. Never recruit players who have "Little League" or overbearing parents. They will kill you!

5. Recruit players who have a deep passion for the game.

6. Don't recruit local players unless you are sure that they can start for you.

7. Too many local players will create big problems for you and the stability of your team.

8. Never over recruit at one position or you will have conflict and cohesion problems.

9. Don't ever compromise your values for the sake of a recruit or you will never have a restful night.

10. Don't make your bed with anyone you don't want to see in the morning.

11. Don't ever cheat to get a player. If you do, that player is nothing but a future informant.

12. There are thousands of good prospects out there, you just have to go out and find them.

13. Don't be influenced by people who don't matter, such as some media or talk-show types who think they know it all. If they knew what was really going on, they would not be sitting behind a computer and a radio microphone.

14. Listen to your brain and call upon your experience when recruiting someone. Don't be influenced by amateurs and fans or you will end buying tickets and sitting with them.

15. Recruit in places where you have had success, where you are respected, and where you respect people who are involved with the recruit and you know people trust you.

16. If somebody talks about illegal inducements, including money and cars, get away from that person as fast as you can. If you make a pact with the devil you will never forgive yourself.

17. Attitude is just as important as talent. You can improve talent but you will never change someone's attitude.

18. Don't ever promise a prospect that he will be a starter because you never know what will happen.

19. Recruit to the needs of your team whenever possible. Players need to see a window where they might contribute or flourish.

20. Try to recruit coachability and toughness. Soft will never be good enough.

TEXAS DAYS

"Texas was effective because it had five or six players that shot threes. Thus, if the defense didn't guard the three-point line it was a problem, but even if they did, the guards were quick athletes who could drive to the basket or take pull-up shots."

—Travis Mays, Texas guard for Penders in 1989 and 1990 NCAA Tournaments

om Penders' run in the 1988 NCAA Tournament put him at the center of two job searches in early April of that year: Texas and Rutgers. Penders knew he probably could have had the Rutgers job and was very familiar with the Scarlet Knights' program because of his Eastern roots. But he knew little about the University of Texas's basketball program or its potential.

In fact, Texas *men's* basketball was an enigma to most of the country and maybe even to many people in Austin. Basically, the sport had been languishing for the previous six seasons under the direction of Bob Weltlich, who played a half-court style. In addition, to many UT fans, he had an off-putting personality. The Erwin Center was an excellent facility, but there needed to be a competitive and exciting team and a coach with a vibrant personality to draw fans.

After final talks with both former Jacksonville (Florida) University coach Bob Wenzel, who was an assistant for the New Jersey Nets, and Penders, UT figured Penders was the guy to put their basketball program on the map. But he at least wanted to see what he was getting himself into in Austin, where UT football was the biggest game in town. Men's basketball ranked well down the list, certainly behind the Lady Horns' basketball team.

Texas officials flew Penders and his wife, Susie, down to Austin to see the Erwin Center. They took the couple on a car ride right up the tunnel to see the court. In order to escape a prying television cameraman, there also was a wild ride to Barton Creek Golf Course and Hotel with UT associate athletic director Craig Helwig at the wheel. They never did manage to lose the television cameraman, but he never got Penders on tape, either.

The Tom Penders era began the next day at the press conference in the Orange Room at the Erwin Center. The Penders era would last ten years and create more flamboyance and excitement than anything Texas basketball had seen in its previous eighty-two years. "He had a flair about him that made people pay attention to him," said Lance Blanks, a Texas guard from 1988 to 1990 and now general manager of the NBA's Phoenix Suns. "I still get comments from people: '*You* played with those other two guards (Travis Mays and Joey Wright) and for Coach Tom Penders.'"

Alvin Heggs, a forward who starred for Penders just one season in 1988–89, but now is a highly respected and very successful part owner of a car dealership in the Houston area, added, "Watching him coming from up North, he was the first white guy whom I had seen with the curl. And those boots on, with that curl—I just think he was driven from a whole 'nother breed."

Penders never said one bad word about Weltlich. He never had to say anything. People in Austin and the fans could tell he was a different cat. In comparison to Weltlich, he was Jay Leno, a laugh-a-minute, 180-degree turn from the previous stern coach. And with a running style, and quips a minute, the turnstiles started to click.

During his first season, Penders made more than 150 public appearances. He rode in parades and appeared at the rodeo. He spoke all over the state at banquets, luncheons, breakfasts, and alumni functions.

The Penders' daughter Karli, who dressed as a UT cheerleader on the sidelines from the age of five through elementary school, remembers the increasing awareness of UT basketball. "My teachers would ask me about the games and be as excited as I was after wins," Karli recalls. "Longhorn basketball t-shirts were becoming a standard uniform at my school. I was even excused to travel with the team on occasion."

"We had so much to prove," said Travis Mays, a star guard on those early Penders teams at UT and now an assistant women's basketball coach at LSU. "We were not in a power conference. We had to travel to every Rec center and school in Austin to beat people to prove how good we were. They would say, 'The women draw more than you.' No doubt he was the perfect guy to come in. Tom had a quiet swagger about him. He was the cool dude who would say things under his breath."

"When I went to Austin in 1988–89 the Horns had drawn about 4,000 a game the season before, including the band, cheerleaders, security, and season-ticket holders who rarely showed up," Penders said. "In my first season, we were number one in the country in attendance increase (average of more than 5,983 fans for 14 games), as we averaged over 10,000 fans a game."

The style had a lot to do with it as well. Austin is not a haven for basketball purists, who preferred a 1950s-style game. Maybe the UT fans could stomach low-scoring football games, if UT won. But basketball was different. Because he had the athletes at guard to run, Penders unleashed them and played to the crowd.

"It was ironic. I had watched Rhode Island the year before in the NCAA Tournament," Blanks said. "They had upset some teams and challenged Duke. I really thought what a fun style to play in. And then DeLoss Dodds (Texas athletic director) goes out and hires Tom. I had positive thoughts about his style.

"I remember (later) watching the opponents' eyes, and they would almost have this expression, 'He shot *that?*'"

"That was night and day," Mays said of the difference between Weltlich and Penders. "I felt if Tom Penders hadn't become the coach I never would have had an opportunity to be a pro, get the records I did, or become the player I became. Not anything bad about him (Weltlich), but it is a fact. We were so limited in what we could show. He (Penders) opened it up and we could show our skill sets and show how competitive we were. It was night-and-day contrast between the coaches."

Penders had already gotten a partial scouting report on his new team during the 1988 Final Four from former Oklahoma and SMU coach Dave Bliss, who had just taken the New Mexico job. As the Mustangs' coach, Bliss had coached against Texas in the Southwest Conference.

"He was a friend of Weltlich's. Knowing Weltlich had already gone, I asked him what he thought of the Texas job," Penders recalled. "He said Texas had who he thought was the best player in the conference in Travis Mays. They had a couple of big slow guys, one from Brazil (Jose Nassar) and one from Ohio (George Muller). And they had a kid sitting out, Texas High School Player of the Year (Lance Blanks). I don't think he even knew about Joey Wright (sitting out after transferring from Drake). Bliss said, 'Tom, they will love your style of play down there. You may not be able to win right away, but you have these great players.'"

The returning players took to Penders quickly. Heggs had been a reserve under Weltlich in 1987–88. "The first thing he said to me that year, 'Big fellow, you will be starting,'" Heggs said. "Tom Penders turned it around. He did not have all these restrictions. He told us you will have more fun playing basketball than you have ever had in your life. I don't understand how a team could be 16–14 and then 25–9 the next year with the same players. Tom Penders brings something mentally different, the way you approach things."

Heggs, Blanks, and Mays all said Penders had to push them to shoot more because the more restrictive style of Weltlich had made them hesitant to put the ball up. "We were in Hawaii and I was not shooting a high percentage," Mays said of games early in the 1988–89 season, Penders' first in Austin. "He pulled me over at a timeout and said, 'If my number one player is not going to shoot it, I have a spot on the bench for you.' I never stopped shooting.

"Even if the three-point line was not there, you still had freedom to shoot with Tom," Mays added. "He instilled confidence. At his first press conference at UT, he said, 'I am going to tell you what we want you to do—get up and down floor.' He knew what he was doing. He motivated us. He said we would run after timeouts, after TV timeouts, and out of the locker room. He would get your juices flowing to be the best you could be."

Penders led the Horns on tournament runs during his first two seasons in Texas, developing a sense of excitement in Austin. The Horns' 1989–90 NCAA Tournament run is detailed in Chapter 5. In Penders' first season of 1988–89, the Horns scored more than one hundred points ten times. In his second season, they went over the century mark eleven times. In Weltlich's previous six seasons, Texas never scored one hundred points.

This revved-up offensive production set the stage for a basketball renaissance in terms of wins over a ten-year period, although Penders wouldn't always run like the first two seasons. He started to get great players who could win playing different styles.

Penders' initial running style started filling the Erwin Center, putting UT on national television and eventually attracting in-state recruits. Penders believes the slow-down styles of several Southwest Conference teams inhibited the ability of the league to get good recruits. Also, the SWC's Raycom television package would put some of the most dreadful games of the week on the air.

"Texas Christian University coach Moe Iba, when I first got to the league, said our style would never float in the SWC," Penders said. "I didn't really know Moe. I respected Moe a lot, but his style of basketball was totally opposite of mine. He was *all* half court. He wanted the game in the fifties and sixties, and I wanted to play in the nineties or hundreds when I got to Texas. I just said we will have to wait and see. Gerald Myers of Texas Tech made the same comment as Moe did.

"Shelby Metcalf at Texas A&M, said, 'Ah, this is the way the game should be played.' And Nolan Richardson of Arkansas said, 'I love the way Tom's teams play.' But there were a lot of coaches in the league that loved the half-court game, which almost invariably ended up being a free-throw shooting contest.

"Because of that style of play, Texas kids were leaving to play in the ACC, the Big Eight, the Big Ten, the SEC. The top players were going everywhere but the SWC. After two years of us playing in the nineties, we had a tremendous impact on that. When Texas and Arkansas played like it was a track meet, the whole country stopped and watched."

Starting with the 1989–90 season Penders also started working at getting Texas games on national television through his East Coast contacts. "One of the most important factors in today's recruiting is the conference that you play in and how much exposure [television] does your conference get," Penders said. "That's why ESPN is so powerful. If you are not on ESPN on a regular basis the top players have no interest. That eventually killed SWC basketball. In the 1980s the SWC had an opportunity to be part of *Monday Night College Hoops*, now known as *Big Monday*.

"The powers that be turned down ESPN for reasons that still are not clear. Ignorance, stupidity, and lack of foresight are good guesses. They opted to stay with their Raycom weekly Saturday afternoon package that brought in pennies and nickels and low ratings. All you could hear were squeaking sneakers, whistles—lots of whistles—and bouncing basketballs. That didn't help recruiting."

Throughout the early 1990s Penders was able to secure Arkansas–Texas and Texas–Houston games on ABC or ESPN and pepper his non-conference schedule with a few games ESPN, ABC, or CBS would pick up to supplement the SWC schedule . . . Cal–Santa Barbara, Oklahoma, Connecticut, Georgia, Utah, LSU, Florida, North Carolina. Penders' final two seasons (1996–98) were spent in the Big 12 Conference. But by that time, Penders had turned the tide in recruiting and had started getting some of the top players.

When Penders first arrived in Austin, he basically had an out-of-state roster that Weltlich had recruited. Initially, he had to go to the junior colleges to fill in holes with such players as Bahamian forwards Locksley Collie and Dexter Cambridge, and Panama center Guillermo Myers from Lon Morris College in east Texas.

"As we started to win at Texas we were able to recruit the state of Texas (high schools)," Penders said. "Over my last seven years at Texas we averaged around ten players a year from the state of Texas. We had a couple of players from Houston, a few more from the Dallas–Fort Worth metroplex area. And we still kept recruiting junior college players from east Texas like Dennis Jordan and Ira

Clark from Temple Junior College.

Texas plucked high school big man Albert Burditt out of Austin, a player Georgetown, Michigan, and North Carolina were all recruiting. Gabe Muoneke, another standout big man from Houston, signed on at Texas. Then guards Kris Clack and Chico Vazquez, also from Austin, came into the fold as freshmen. Clack was the first McDonald's All-American to sign with the Longhorns.

Once Penders had the Longhorns established, some Texas high school players returned to Texas from other universities: Freeport's Rich McIver from Michigan, Clute's Tremaine Wingfield from Louisville, Port Arthur's B. J. Tyler from DePaul. Those players, dissatisfied with their situations at those schools, *called* Texas and asked if the school would take them if they transferred.

"Joey Meyer, the coach at DePaul, played a half-court game," Penders recalled about Tyler's decision to transfer. "And B. J. was a racehorse. And he wasn't happy there. And it was cold. When we went up and played DePaul and beat them, B. J. had already quit the team. He was going to transfer back. Where he was going was up in the air. But he told us he wanted to come to Texas. He was not New York City flashy. But he could dribble in and outside his legs and was lightening fast. He was a great outside shooter, who would pass it. Basically, he made good decisions and was lightening quick on both ends of the floor."

In the early 1990s, Penders had made the Erwin Center, complete with a pre-game laser show, a raucous place to be. So the grass was no longer always greener out of state. "The crowd (at the Erwin Center) was absolutely phenomenal," said Tony Barone, Texas A&M's coach at the time. "No one in the league (Arkansas already had left for the SEC) approximates this. The noise level was an intimidating factor. I told my kids after the game, 'This is what big-time college basketball is all about.'"

Texas Tech forward Darvin Ham added, "When people think about the Southwest Conference, the first team that comes to mind is Texas. They have a great national reputation, and they play a fun style of basketball. So that's a game I get up for the most."

After Arkansas left for the SEC following the 1990–91 season, the Longhorns and Penders probably never got the recognition nor the higher NCAA seeds they deserved because of the conference's perceived mediocrity without the powerhouse Arkansas program.

Texas and Penders' last three seasons (1993–94 to 1995–96) before the SWC broke up resulted in two regular-season SWC titles and two post-season tournament crowns. After failing to make the NCAA Tournament during an injury-riddled 1992–93 season, Texas made the next three NCAA tournaments (1994–96) as a member of the SWC, but never entered the tournament better than a six seed.

The Longhorns also were an eleven seed in 1995 and number ten in 1996 and never advanced past the second round because they were playing powerhouse teams in the second round: Michigan, Maryland, and Wake Forest. Had they been in a better conference they probably would have had easier tournament paths as higher seeds.

In 1994, after the sixth-seeded Longhorns beat eleventh-seeded Western Kentucky in the first round, they gave the three seed, Michigan's "Fab Five," all they wanted, 84–79, before losing.

"The 1993–94 team was my best at Texas, in guard B. J. Tyler's senior year," Penders said. "We went through the Southwest Conference that year winning by an average of twenty points per game. We had only two loses in conference play—a one-pointer at Texas A&M and a double-overtime loss at Texas Tech. We had great guards with (Tyler, Roderick Anderson, Terrence Rencher) an excellent frontcourt of Tremaine Wingfield, Albert Burditt, Rich McIver, and other good bench guys. We had tremendous depth.

"My son (Tommy) was on that team. And he played sparingly, but he was a great free-throw shooter at the end of games. We never lost games where we had a lead. We were very quick and a great pressing team. We could beat you in a lot of different ways. A lot of teams that we had shot great from three-point range, but had no inside game. This team had an inside game. Reggie Freeman was a freshman, and by the end of the year he was a pretty good contributor."

A year later, Texas was getting no respect in the NCAA Tournament again after claiming both the 1995 SWC regular-season co-championship and the post-season tournament crown. The Longhorns were an eleven seed playing sixth-seeded Oregon. UT, however, won going away. "That was the most unorthodox game I have ever been affiliated with in my years of coaching basketball," said a shocked Oregon coach Jerry Green. "Their defense dictates so much of the game and I haven't seen anything like that at Kansas or here, or at North Carolina. I think Tom has done a great job of using the talent that he has got. What they do, and the style they play is very, very unusual, and they do it excellently."

Penders had successfully orchestrated another upset with his strategy. "I knew our press would really bother Oregon because they only had one ball-handler," Penders said. "Instead of trapping the second pass, as soon as their point guard got it we came right at him, hemmed him in, made him give it up and wouldn't let him get it back. They would have to have their shooting guard dribble the ball down the floor, having to make a decision. He was a great scorer, but he was not a good decision maker. Soon they got running with us. They never got into a good rhythm."

In the 1996 NCAA Tournament, as a ten seed, Penders' Longhorns upset seventh-seeded Michigan, 80–76, this time. "You don't beat a Michigan or lead a Wake Forest for thirty-nine minutes and not be a top fifteen team," Penders said. "For all the doubters, we showed we could compete with the big boys. Not many people figured we would make it here."

And when the Big 12 was formed and started competition in 1996–97, Texas didn't miss a beat. The Longhorns finally were playing in a strong league with the old Big Eight Conference, plus Texas A&M, Texas Tech, and Baylor. Because of the increased competition and television visibility of the Big 12, Penders was able to put together his best recruited group that included Austin high school star, seven-foot Chris Mihm, local standout Luke Axtell, an Austin Westlake teammate of Mihm's, and guard Bernard Smith from Conroe.

"Some of my good friends in the Big Eight thought we were going slumming in basketball, but that's not true," Oklahoma State coach Eddie Sutton said. "I told them the University of Texas and Texas Tech could come in right now and play with us. And that was certainly proven last year (1996–97)."

In 1996–97, the first year of the Big 12 operations, Texas finished tied for third in the conference standings and advanced to the Sweet 16 of the NCAA Tournament. If Penders had been allowed to continue coaching at UT, who knows what might have happened with those recruits. Penders has been gone for more than twelve years now, and millions of dollars have been poured into Texas basketball. There are still no National Championship banners hanging from the rafters of the Erwin Center.

STYLE AND STRATEGY CHANGES

As he had done earlier in his career at the different stops, Penders changed styles depending on the personnel at Texas. "We used the three pointer when we had the Blanks–Mays–Wright backcourt," Penders added. "We averaged more than ninety points a game in my first two seasons at Texas. My third season we became a bruising inside team with Panama Myers, Locksley Collie, Dexter Cambridge, and Albert Burditt as the focus. We were a bad three-point-shooting team. But we had Dexter, Locksley, and Panama and we led the league in rebounding. Joey Wright was our only consistent three-point shooter. We didn't press as much or run as much as usual, but we did not turn the ball over."

"All you have to do is go back to Fordham," said Penders' son Tommy. "I remember games there of 47–45. At Texas, the third year we got down and dirty. Then when Chico Vazquez was point guard, and we went to the Sweet 16 (in 1997), he played more of a half-court game. At George Washington, the year we went to the NCAA Tournament in 1999, we went inside to the post. He changed throughout the years. He won at Columbia and did not run and gun."

Penders' reputation as a run-and-gun coach was probably the most misunderstood thing about him. His coaching style adapted to his players. And his methods stood up through different regions, different eras of play, different decades, and with different players from all over the country and from different schools: private schools, city schools, small towns, schools in the suburbs, and elsewhere.

The three-point shot became a major weapon for Penders at Rhode Island and early at Texas when it came into the game starting with the 1986–87 season. But it would have been stupid not to exploit the rule, if a coach had players who made three pointers at a high percentage.

"If you shoot 37 percent from three-point range that is like 60 percent from two-point range," Penders said. "And if you are shooting threes, you have a better chance of getting the rebounds, because they go long (and your guards are out there to pick them up)."

Mays said shooting the three pointer at Texas made the game fun and the players ran past opponents just to get the shot. But, he added, Penders had a method to this perceived chaos. "As players we ran the floor because we knew at the end we could shoot it," Mays said. "You would not get wings to run the floor—unless they could shoot it. With that offense we put so much pressure on the defense, we were able to attack before the defense got set. People thought it was helter-skelter, but we practiced it."

Penders had a staple of not turning the ball over, playing hard, getting after the other team, and having fun.

Blanks said, "I took many things from Tom Penders:

- Have confidence in yourself and in your players.

- Balance and focus on what you have to do from a technical standpoint.

- Enjoy what you are doing; he kept us energized and loose.

- Management of his players; he knew which buttons to push. He had a nice way about him with his words and language.

"He took us to a much higher level than if he had not been there."

"I am going to tell you, I don't think many coaches out there have a total package as far as being a motivator and an instiller of confidence, great father figure, and could handle the Xs and Os," Mays added. "He is going to tell you what you are going to do, then you have to go in the gym and maximize your skill sets. He wasn't a coach who would tell you what you couldn't do. He told me what I could do and I have taken that with me. He told me I could compete with anybody in country and play with them. And he let me prove that I could."

Texas blended the New York City kids with the Texas talent, and UT became a tough basketball team. There is a work ethic that Penders has always developed with his teams at all his stops.

"I only recruited two players from New York during my ten years at Texas," Penders said. "But they just happened to be two of the greatest players in UT history. Terrence Rencher, a six-foot-three lefty from the Bronx, became the leading scorer in Texas and SWC history and Reggie Freeman, who was a star as well.

"They led the other kids. New York City players played year-round and didn't even think about playing another sport. Texas kids, if a gym wasn't air conditioned or there wasn't an organized team, they wouldn't play. New York City kids lived on pick-up basketball. They incorporated that kind of work ethic and attitude at Texas."

Looking back at the Penders era at Texas, eight NCAA Tournament appearances in ten years was by far the best decade of UT basketball up until that point. Penders came to Austin to set a foundation from which others could build programs. That foundation was absent in Austin until Penders arrived on the scene.

WINDING DOWN:
PENDERS-DELOSS DODDS RELATIONSHIP

The Penders and Dodds were as close as two families could be. In fact, the Texas athletic department "extended family" routinely would have barbeques at coaches' and UT athletic officials' homes during the summer on a rotating basis. Penders and Dodds were a subset of this for nearly a decade. Once you were in the inner-circle of Texas athletics you pretty much knew everything about everybody in the department. These people even took vacations together. Recreation and business deals were intertwined.

In the May of 1991, the Penders and Dodds were on one of these getaways in the fashionable Colorado mountain resort of Beaver Creek, about one hundred miles from Denver. The two couples were staying with a powerful University of Texas booster from Dallas, Mike Myers, who had a house just off the slopes of where the Southwest Conference was holding a meeting at the Beaver Creek Hyatt. DeLoss Dodds loved golf as much as he did his wife, Mary Ann. And Penders was known to swing a pretty mean golf club in his day as well. It was a perfect plot.

Between swings, some serious things were being discussed, however. While Arkansas was in the process of leaving the SWC and moving to the Southeastern Conference, Penders also was considering a possible move to the NBA and the New York Knicks. He was one of three serious candidates for the job, including NBC television commentator Pat Riley (who would ultimately get it), and Doug Collins. It would basically boil down to Penders and Riley.

In Colorado, Penders was fielding frequent calls in Myers' house from New York Knicks executives Ernie Grunfeld and Dave Checketts, who were wooing his services. They liked his fast-paced basketball style, his Eastern roots, and the fact as a college coach he probably wouldn't want to usurp their power in the front office as the NBA–savvy Riley might.

But back to the subways and rush? Why?

Penders had just completed his third season at Texas and had been to three straight NCAA Tournaments. Austin was comfortable. The Penders' spacious stone home in the Rollingwood section of Austin was several times the size of anything they could have afforded in New York City, where they had a postage-stamp-size apartment when he was at Fordham. When they got married in 1980 in the chapel on the Fordham campus, they went to the Bahamas for their honeymoon and had so little money to spend they joked about heading to happy hour for the free conch fritters to survive.

If he got the Knicks job, they obviously would be able to upgrade in their dwellings and have more disposable income. Still, life was good in Austin and the dollar went a lot further than in New York City. And with Arkansas leaving the conference where they had won the three previous titles, Penders and Texas were set up to be the dominant team in the SWC if it could hang together. Penders didn't really want to leave, and his contract at Texas was currently being negotiated for more money. At this point and time, Penders actually could help DeLoss with *his* contract.

The spring of 1991 was long before the UT football renaissance under Mack Brown would begin in 1998. Dodds was not viewed as the wunderkind athletic director he is today. He was hardly an architect of UT football success. In fact, his very job status was unclear. Certainly, Penders was his star hire in the two major sports, bold-faced on Dodds' résumé in case he needed it.

UT football was not where anybody in Austin wanted it. And to some extent Dodds' hands were tied regarding the hires. UT had claimed the SWC football title in 1990, but a 46–3 loss in the 1991 Cotton Bowl put a damper on the season. Head football coach David McWilliams, who was hired more by the UT old guard than Dodds, would last only another season and be replaced by a UT presidential hire, John Mackovic, who would coach the Longhorns through another six years of up and down seasons.

Dodds needed a life raft in 1991 for the current and impending rocky waters he was about to encounter before Mack Brown's arrival after the 1997 football season.

"I asked DeLoss about his contract," Penders recalled of a conversation. "And he said it was up in the air. I told him I didn't want to leave Texas, but I wanted to work for him. I asked him if I should call President Bill Cunningham and tell him about the Knicks and ask about your contract."

Penders did just that. And President Cunningham agreed to get both deals done. So, in effect, Penders struck the deal that led Dodds to security in that era. Penders turned down the Knicks and stayed. Dodds stayed. And Texas basketball continued to enjoy the good times.

Off and on, Penders was getting offers to leave Austin because of the success he was having during the 1990s. But the offer that really mattered was in the spring of 1997 as Penders was taking the Longhorns to the NCAA Tournament Sweet 16. Remember Rutgers?

Well, the Scarlet Knights had wound up with Wenzel after Penders turned them down in 1988. And Wenzel coached for a decade until getting fired. Now, Rutgers was coming after Penders again and got turned down again. Penders got a more lucrative contract at Texas.

In the process, the relationship between Dodds and Penders changed because Penders had had to reach above Dodds to get his contract approved. And with Penders' health problems in the fall of 1997, the coach admitted he didn't know that he could even take a sabbatical for fear of being in violation of his contract and being terminated. So he missed only two games and coached through the rest of the 1997–98 season with his newly implanted defibrillator.

With the new recruits and a young team, Texas was up and down but finished strong in the Big 12 Post-Season Tournament. And with most of the team returning, the Longhorns would be a power the following season and the Penders era would move into its eleventh season at UT. Penders was still adjusting to life with a defibrillator and trying to stay alive.

"That spring, it was the first year we hadn't gone to the NCAA Tournament since 1993," Susie Penders said. "I thought it would be a good time to take a break so I suggested we take Karli (their daughter) somewhere for spring break. We were members of RCI, a time-share vacation exchange, but the only place I could find at such late notice was out of the country. We got five days at this resort on the island of St. Martin."

Before he left, Penders tied up loose ends in the office. And he also received an interesting visitor. "Bob Utley, a big UT booster, came by my office right before we went on the trip," Penders said. "He said, 'Tom, with your health, you don't need this. A good friend of mine Tom Hicks, a UT regent, has bought Host Communications. Whatever you are making he will be willing to pay you.' I told him I am fifty-two and didn't want to quit coaching and thanked him. That same day, DeLoss called me down to his office and told me that some of my players, four to be exact, came to him and said they wanted to transfer. In disbelief, I said, 'Let's get them in here.' We were able to get a hold of three of the four players, and none of them said they were unhappy or that they were going to transfer. It was quite the opposite; they were all very friendly and seemed totally content. When none of the players contacted had a problem with me, I left for the trip thinking everything was cool. Later on I found out that the meeting had taken place almost a week earlier, and that a couple of the players didn't even know why they were being driven to the home of the athletic director. Not only was I chafed to find out that my AD had a meeting with some of my players without my knowledge, but he waited almost a week until the day I was to depart on a trip to tell me, and I had to find out from the media when the meeting actually took place." Keep in mind the Penders were staying at isolated St. Martin Island in the Caribbean. The condo unit they were occupying did not have direct-calling phones. The resort had only a switchboard where people could call into the room. The nearest pay phone was two miles away. This was before cell phones were common. And Penders did not have one. He couldn't even use his UT phone credit card on the island. So basically, he and Susie were cut off from what was going on in Austin. The Internet was not even a factor yet.

This was supposed to be a relaxing, stress-free vacation for Penders, the recovering heart patient. Assistant Coach Eddie Oran and the office secretary were told to handle everything but an emergency.

"That's when all that stuff happened (when the study hall attendance record was mentioned on the radio in Austin)," Penders said of his absence. "The lone switchboard operator at the resort couldn't keep up with all of the calls coming in wanting to get through to our room. There were people—friends, alumni, the media—all trying to alert me to what the *Austin American-Statesman* (the local newspaper) was reporting and to get my response. Those few that finally got through had been on hold for hours. The switchboard operator was ready to quit. I was told there were headlines claiming verbal abuse, a clandestine meeting at the home of the athletic director, violation of the Buckley Amendment (referring to the unauthorized release of a students' grades), and I had no idea what was going on there. But then things started adding up—the strange visit and offer from Bob Utley, a close friend and confidante of Dodds, rumors being "leaked" to the *Austin American-Statesman*—and I asked myself was I being set up? Forced out?"

The media jumped on this like a pack of wolves, all hoping to get the Pulitzer Prize for Investigative Journalism. All the while the Penders were isolated in St. Martin. As Penders learned, once the media latches on to an idea for a story, the truth often becomes irrelevant. The controversy that the Penders returned to had taken on a life of its own.

"And when we got back to Austin, we were having to orchestrate our own press conferences on my front lawn," Penders said. "I'm having to answer questions about verbal abuse and the Buckley Amendment. My star players were dragged into the controversy, standing up to defend me on their own. They called their own press conference. Meanwhile, DeLoss wouldn't speak with me directly. I couldn't even go into my office. A UT alum and attorney, Joe Longley, advised me to get a lawyer. Joe introduced me to Roy Minton, a highly respected Austin attorney. After speaking with my assistant Eddie Oran, Minton agreed to represent me. Roy advised me that the university had no grounds to terminate me, and he wanted to know if I wanted to continue to work under the existing conditions. I felt the breach between DeLoss and I had become too wide, and I authorized Minton to negotiate a fair settlement on my behalf. It was a circus for two or three weeks. Because I got through all that, I guess my heart *was* better.

Shortly thereafter, Penders reached a settlement with Texas, which included about $900,000 in cash and the aforementioned media job with Host Communications, making the total buyout about $2.4 million—should he not take another coaching job. Penders indeed returned to coach at two institutions—George Washington and Houston—who fully checked out his credentials and what happened during the final days at Texas.

"I worked at Texas for ten wonderful years and for the most part DeLoss Dodds and I had a great relationship," Penders said. "As a matter of fact, I consider him to be a friend except for a few weeks in March 1998. We traveled together, raised millions of dollars together, and shared family trips to Colorado. We 'divorced' in April of 1998 for reasons I still have no clue about.

"It was too good to be true, but like all divorces both parties share part of the blame. I think I took DeLoss for granted after awhile. But I was never disloyal to him while I worked for him. We spent ten years together, and that's longer than the average marriage. He was a solid athletic director. We didn't always agree, but I know we had tremendous respect for each other. I probably stayed at Texas too long, but my family loved Austin and my son played for me and graduated at UT. Two of my nieces also graduated from UT. It was a hard place to walk away from, and I had numerous opportunities at the NBA and college level to leave. But I didn't want to depart. I had built a great program, and I still have many wonderful friendships there.

"I have moved forward with my life. There were no rules violations and no real scandal. UT honored my contract. And DeLoss and I have buried the hatchet. Texas gave me a great opportunity, and I will never be able to repay him and the University of Texas. It didn't end the way I wanted it to end, but that's how it goes."

It didn't take long for Penders to land another job in the spring of 1998—just a matter of weeks. Old friend and competitor Jack Kvancz, the athletic director at George Washington University, convinced Penders that he could win immediately at GW. And he did. Penders' first George Washington team won the Atlantic 10 Conference West Division, compiled a 20–9 record, and went to the 1999 NCAA Tournament (Penders' third school to do so).

Penders inherited a diverse group of players at George Washington, which was an international school. The team resembled the United Nations with players from several countries: Spain, Israel, the Netherlands, Portugal, Russia, Canada, and the Central African Republic. But Penders' best player on that 1998–99 team hailed from nearby Baltimore—guard Shawnta Rogers.

"He stood five foot three on a dry day in August," Penders said of the Atlantic 10's leading scorer. "Pound for pound, inch for inch, he is one of the best basketball players that I've ever seen. Every team we played tried to play special defenses against Shawnta, but nobody could stop him. He had no weaknesses in his game. And he was a great shooter who could always get his shot off. "

Mike King, a six-foot-five sophomore who played in the same backcourt with Rogers in high school, joined him to form a terrific backcourt for GW. Forward Yegor Mescheriakov from Belarus, Russia, was the other star. Penders only had a couple of scholarships to offer for the next season, and he recruited two players from the Washington, D.C., area—guards SirValiant Brown and Chris Monroe. And they carried the team during the rest of Penders' three-year tenure there.

Brown, as a freshman, was the second leading scorer in the country (24.6 points per game) during Penders' second season (15–15) in 1999–2000 when the Colonials set a school record for scoring in a season. Monroe would go on to become the school's all-time leading scorer. Penders coached one more season at GW in 2000–01 when the team (14–18) advanced to the semifinals of the Atlantic 10 post-season tournament before losing to eventual champion Temple, 77–76.

After that 2000–01 season, Penders believed his health was of the utmost concern and told Kvancz he needed to step aside to take care of it. At a press conference after the season with Penders present, Kvancz said: "It was after the Temple game, when we missed that last foul shot that could have won the game for us, that I really noticed a difference (in Penders). It dawned on me that he had been doing this over thirty years (including high school at that point). And in the weeks after the Atlantic 10 Tournament, I sensed he was tired. As I look at him, I said there is a man who exudes class, and he can coach the game of basketball."

PENDERS' TEXAS LEGACY

Although Penders and Dodds appear to have buried the horns (their differences) more than a decade later, Penders has yet to be formally recognized for basically transforming UT basketball into a big-time operation after the Weltlich era.

Maybe it is just a matter of time before someone in Austin will honor Penders. But more than twelve years have passed since that hectic spring of 1998 when Penders departed amid controversy that resulted in his settlement with UT for the four years remaining on his contract.

Two of Penders' most prominent players during his years at UT—guards Travis Mays and Lance Blanks—have been inducted into the University of Texas Men's Athletics Hall of Honor in 2002 and 2007 respectively. Chris Mihm, who played for Penders his last season of 1997–98, is in the 2010 Class. The Penders have never been invited back by the school to help them enjoy the honors. But they have been invited by the players to sit at their tables. Tom was present for Mays' induction ceremony, and Susie attended in 2007 as a guest of Blanks. Sad, but true.

Penders sent DeLoss Dodds a note after Blanks was inducted in 2007. And Dodds returned a note to Penders saying:

Tom,
Thanks for the note. It was good to see and visit with Susie. I got the update on your kids—it's fun to see them grow. The best to you and your Cougars.
Sincerely,
DeLoss

Penders has been active getting others into the Texas Men's

Athletics Hall of Honor, including helping former UT basketball coach Abe Lemons make it in 1994. Penders also brought Lemons back to talk to his UT teams as he later did with former Cougar coach Guy Lewis at Houston.

"Tom has always paid respect to former coaches," Susie said. "At the University of Houston, he made every effort to visit with Coach Lewis, his wife Dina, and daughter Sherry after every home game. Sherry always told us how much it meant to her mom and dad."

Now, Penders' former players believe it is time he is honored as well. "I think relative to its basketball history and his (Penders') legacy, the school should have some place in the University Hall of Honor," Blanks said. "It would be hard to rival what he did. Not many coaches (at UT) could rival the success he had, especially after the dormant period. Certainly things took a turn for the better. . . . My guess is that some day he will be in there."

"I think he should have been in the first day he could have been inducted," Penders' former player Alvin Heggs said. "If you don't induct somebody who brought basketball back to Texas, then there is something wrong.

"Consider the first year I got there—the Erwin Center. There were 4,000 people in the stands in an arena that holds around 16,000 people, " Heggs added. "Then, to turn it around Coach Penders' first year to have more than 10,000 a game and to have some sellouts, that's even more incredible. That started in 1988 and went on until 1998. All those guys (since) have benefited and Rick Barnes has benefited. And if they don't put him (Penders) in there, then shame on them."

In 2006, the University of Texas listed the Top 100 Moments in the first one hundred years of Longhorn basketball on its website. And Penders' teams and players were mentioned nineteen times.

UT TOP 100
FROM THE PENDERS ERA

MOMENT NO. 9

March 22, 1990: Texas rallies from a 16-point deficit with 18:55 left (57–41) to top No. 25 Xavier 102–89 in a NCAA Regional semifinal at Reunion Arena in Dallas. Lance Blanks scores 26 of his 28 points in the second half to lead the comeback. Travis Mays posts a game-high 32 points, while Joey Wright adds 26 in the winning effort. The victory advanced the Horns to the "Elite Eight" for the first time since the tournament expanded to 64 teams.

MOMENT NO. 14

March 18, 1990: Guillermo "Panama" Myers blocks a field-goal attempt by Tony Jones to preserve a 73–72 upset over No. 10 Purdue in a NCAA Second Round game at the RCA Dome in Indianapolis. Travis Mays converted two free throws with seven seconds left to give the Horns a one-point advantage heading into the final sequence. With the win, UT advanced to the NCAA "Sweet 16" for the first time since the tourney expanded to 64 teams.

MOMENT NO. 18

March 3, 1991: In No. 3 Arkansas' final regular-season game as a member of the Southwest Conference, Texas posts a 99–86 upset before a sellout crowd at the Erwin Center. UT defeats the highest AP ranked opponent at home in school history. Texas trailed 61–47 with 17:39 left before storming back to end Arkansas' hopes of an undefeated SWC regular season. The victory also marked the first time in school history that UT had recorded at least 20 wins in three consecutive seasons.

MOMENT NO. 19

March 16, 1990: Travis Mays posts 44 points to lead the 10th-seeded Longhorns to a 100–88 victory against No. 7 seed Georgia in a NCAA First Round game at the RCA Dome in Indianapolis. Mays' 44 points remain a school record for most points in a NCAA Tournament contest. He converted 23-of-27 free throws during the game. His marks for free throws made and free throws attempted are still tied for the most ever in a NCAA Tournament game.

MOMENT NO. 30

1990 NBA Draft: The UT backcourt combo of Travis Mays (No. 14 by Sacramento Kings) and Lance Blanks (No. 26 by Detroit Pistons) are both selected in the first round of the 1990 NBA Draft. It marks just the fourth time in NBA Draft history (to that point in time) that two guards from the same team were taken in the first round.

MOMENT NO. 34

March 16, 1995: Terrence Rencher tallies 19 points in a 90–73 win against Oregon in the First Round of the NCAA Tournament to become the all-time leading scorer in UT history. Rencher concludes his four-year career with 2,306 points in 124 games.

MOMENT NO. 36

Dec. 29, 1993: Tremaine Wingfield hits a 15-footer with 0.2 seconds left in the second overtime to give Texas a 93–91 victory against Utah at the Erwin Center. Wingfield also converted an 18-footer as time expired in regulation to send the game into overtime. Both shots came off length-of-the-court passes from Tommy Penders. The play at the end of regulation began with 0.2 on the clock, while the play in the second overtime began with 1.4 on the clock. The following spring, the NCAA ruled that the only way a team could score on a play that begins with 0.3 or less on the clock is by a tip-in off the inbounds pass.

MOMENT NO. 42

March 17, 1989: Travis Mays scores a team-high 23 points as No. 11 seed Texas upsets sixth-seeded Georgia Tech 76–70 in a NCAA First Round game at Reunion Arena in Dallas. The victory marks the first NCAA Tournament win for the Longhorns in 17 years, since an 85–74 win against No. 19 Houston on March 11, 1972.

MOMENT NO. 45

Mar. 11, 1995: In a contest considered by many to be the greatest game in Southwest Conference history, the Longhorns post a 107–104 overtime win against Texas Tech to win the SWC Tournament title. Freshman Brandy Perryman hit a clutch three-pointer to tie the game at 92–92 with 14 seconds left in regulation, and Terrence Rencher blocked a last-second field goal attempt by Mark Davis to force overtime. The Horns did not miss a shot during the extra session en route to their second straight SWC Tournament crown.

MOMENT NO. 48

Feb. 19, 1997: Dennis Jordan tips in an Al Coleman missed jumper with 3.3 seconds left to give Texas a dramatic 57–56 upset over No. 7 Iowa State at the Erwin Center.

MOMENT NO. 54

Feb. 11, 1990: Travis Mays becomes the first player in UT history to reach the 2,000-point plateau on a lay-up with 16:30 left in the first half of an 85–77 win over TCU. Mays finishes his four-year career with 2,279 points in 124 games.

MOMENT NO. 60

March 10, 1989: Travis Mays hits both ends of a one-and-one with three seconds remaining in overtime to give Texas a 93-91 win against SMU in a SWC Tournament quarterfinal contest at Reunion Arena in Dallas. Joey Wright adds 36 points off the bench for the Longhorns, a mark that still stands as the most points scored off the bench in UT history. The Horns went on to beat TCU 93–89 in overtime the following evening in the semifinals, before falling to Arkansas in the SWC Tournament championship game.

MOMENT NO. 62

Dec. 30, 1995: Sonny Alvarado posts 20 points and 14 rebounds to lead Texas to a 74–72 upset of No. 11 North Carolina before a CBS national television audience in Austin. UNC features a pair of future NBA stars in then-sophomores Vince Carter and Antawn Jamison.

MOMENT NO. 71

Mar. 16, 1997: DeJuan "Chico" Vazquez steals an inbounds pass in the closing seconds to seal an 82–81 win against upstart No. 15 seed Coppin State in a NCAA Second Round game in Pittsburgh. With the victory, UT advances to the "Sweet 16" for the second time since the tournament expanded to 64 teams.

MOMENT NO. 72

Dec. 30, 1989: In a homecoming game for Travis Mays (native of Ocala, Fla.), junior guard Joey Wright steals the show by recording 46 points to lead Texas to a 102–82 win at Stetson. The 46 points mark the third-highest single-game total in school history and the second-highest mark in a road contest.

MOMENT NO. 80

Jan. 12, 1997: Senior guard Al Coleman hits a school-record 10 three-pointers (10-of-14) to lead the Longhorns to a 104–63 victory against Kansas State in Austin.

MOMENT NO. 82

Jan. 14, 1989: Joey Wright follows his own miss with a tip-in at the buzzer to give Texas an 88-86 win at Houston before an ESPN national television audience. The Horns go on to earn their first NCAA Tournament bid in ten seasons later that year.

MOMENT NO. 85

Feb. 26, 1992: Terrence Rencher (34 points), B. J. Tyler (33), and Dexter Cambridge (31) combine to score 98 of Texas' 128 points in a 128–108 victory against Oral Roberts in Austin. This marks the only time in school history that three Longhorns record 30 or more points in a single game.

MOMENT NO. 96

Jan. 30, 1992: Terrence Rencher posts 37 points to lead Texas to a 105–94 win at Virginia Commonwealth. The 37 points remain a school freshman record for most points scored in a single game.

JUMPING TO HOUSTON

"I think absolutely he is unique. His coaching genius is he has been able to take a moribund pro-gram and revitalize it. He takes the other guy's players and makes them better. There is a certain genius in that. And he did it over and over again."

—Rick Schwartz, Penders' minor-league baseball teammate and later a news director for Fox Sports Network

By the spring of 2004 Tom Penders had his health in order. Spending three seasons off the bench as a media personality at ESPN and Westwood One Radio had allowed him to understand life better with the defibrillator. His meds and eating habits had meshed with a healthy lifestyle.

"I spent those three years out of coaching training," Penders said of 2001–04. "My cardiologists said I was in much better shape than I had ever been in. So, I started thinking about getting back into coaching one more time. I had had a few feelers, middle people from different schools. I never had had much interest until February of 2004. Low and behold, I talked to Houston."

Penders was interviewed by then-Houston athletic director Dave Maggard in Dayton while Penders was fulfilling his radio duties for Westwood One during the Atlantic 10 Tournament. Maggard wanted to see if Penders still had "fire in his belly" to coach and asked him several questions about his hectic last month at Texas in the spring of 1998 when he resigned.

"Finally, I got up and thanked him for the interview," Penders said. "I knew I could win there, but I was not interested in working for someone who doubted me. I went on to say I did no wrong at Texas and they would not have given me a lucrative settlement if I had done wrong at Texas. I excused myself and headed to the elevator."

Maggard persisted and headed Penders off at the elevator. He seemed to like what he had heard and how Penders had defended himself. A strong proponent for Penders getting the job was Corby Robertson, whose father—former UH Board of Regents member and Athletics Committee Chairman Corbin J. Robertson—helped build UH's athletic program. UH's football stadium is named Robertson Stadium after Corby's father. Penders had developed a friendship with Corby, a former UT linebacker and successful Houston businessman, years ago when Penders was head coach at UT.

After Maggard's due diligence and Robertson's support, among others, Penders was hired as only the seventh basketball coach in school history.

Penders came to Houston in late March 2004 with dreams of getting UH back to the NCAA Tournament for the first time since 1992. It would be no easy task; UH had managed just two winning records in its previous eleven seasons under three different coaches (Alvin Brooks, Clyde Drexler, and Ray McCallum).

"They had been really down and they had never come that close to winning a Conference USA Championship since joining the league in 1996–97," Penders said. "That's a challenge I have always enjoyed. There's nothing more satisfying than turning around a losing program that people have insisted can't be done."

Penders evaluated the player personnel of the three previous Houston coaches, who averaged about ten victories a season. "I began looking at the rosters of those three coaches," Penders said. "Most of the players were local. Alvin Brooks averaged ten Houston players a year on his roster. Clyde Drexler averaged eleven Houston players. Ray McCallum eleven and a half Houston-area players during the previous regime here. They had too many local guys. I like a more diverse roster. And my philosophy has always been to limit the number of local players, unless they are the top players.

"I always believed in mining the areas where I have been successful. I have always been successful in the New York–New Jersey area over my career. I still knew all the big players up in that area. And they knew me."

Drexler had recruited some high-caliber local high school players such as Alton Ford and George Williams, but he still had two losing seasons and won only nineteen games in two years. Penders' predecessor, McCallum, except for guard Lanny Smith, did not have the level of local players who could get Houston into the top half of C-USA.

"That's what I observed on film," Penders said. "Andre Owens, a guard I inherited, was far and away the best player on McCallum's roster. He had been at Indiana as a freshman on Coach Mike Davis's team. Owens and Ray McCallum were both from Indianapolis. And Owens transferred here because of that. The local Houston guys on the film I studied, quite frankly, had not been very impressive."

Penders looked back at the roster of the most recent successful head coach at UH, Pat Foster, who had a 142–73 record from 1986 to 1993 and took UH to three NCAA Tournaments and three NITs in seven seasons. "Pat recruited the junior college players and got transfers and had some success," Penders said. "So I also went to

Louisiana and other places as well as the junior colleges."

The recruiting of legendary UH coach, Guy V. Lewis, who took the Cougars to five Final Fours (1967, 1968, 1982, 1983, 1984), followed a similar pattern. "Guy V. Lewis survived and made his career because he had the foresight to reach into places like New York and Illinois for players like Jack Thompson and Gary Phillips early on and then hit a home run by signing Elvin Hayes from the backwoods of Louisiana and Don Chaney from Baton Rouge," said Penders, who remains close to Lewis.

"Those two not only broke the color barrier down in the South but they also led Houston to Final Fours in 1967 and 1968. Guy V. was a true pioneer who had the guts to leave the local scene and find great talent around the country. Without Hayes and Chaney, Coach Lewis might be a trivia question instead of a five-time Final Four coach."

When Lewis made his last big run from 1982 to 1984 and advanced to three Final Fours, he had a guard, Lynden Rose, from the Bahamas, and then the centerpiece of the team, center Hakeem Olajuwon, from Nigeria. He added to those key parts with the local talent of Clyde Drexler, who actually wasn't that highly recruited, Michael Young, and Larry Micheaux.

As a result, three of the five players Penders signed in the spring of 2004 played immediately and none of the three were from Houston: Brian Latham, combo guard, super defensive player from Memphis out of Midland (Texas) Junior College; forward Sergio de Randamie from Surinam and out of Midland Junior College; and Chris Lawson, six-foot-three guard from Chicago, who played at Los Angeles City College.

In Penders' first season of 2004–05, Houston jumped into the upper echelon of C-USA, won eighteen games, and received an NIT bid. Houston beat a Top 25 team for the first time since the 1996–97 season. The Cougars had lost to twenty-four straight teams ranked in the Top 25. That season the Cougars also led the country in turnover margin (plus 7.5) per game with an emphasis on defense.

"He's got a winning attitude and that is contagious," guard Lanny Smith said during Penders' first season in Houston in 2004–05. "He's so loose, he is always joking around. If we're down with a minute to go in a game, we're not tight."

"The first year can be fun if you feel that your team got the most out of their abilities," Penders said. "We were at least close to doing that. There was a growing sense of pride and our players seemed eager to keep growing. We knocked off number sixteen Louisville in our C-USA opener on ESPN. In February, we beat Memphis by thirteen also on ESPN. We now had set the foundation and we were anxious to build a nice house. A week after the season ended I was awarded a new five-year contract."

In 2005–06, Penders had the personnel to play the gambling, trapping, and switching defense that he loved with new recruits Jahmar Thorpe and guard Oliver Lafayette, who was from Baton Rouge, Louisiana.

Houston made the NIT again, beat Brigham Young in the first round, and lost a buzzer beater at Missouri State in the second round. Houston finished 21–10 and beat two Top 25 teams in a week: number twenty-five LSU in Baton Rouge and number thirteen Arizona in Houston. It was UH's first twenty-win season since 1992–93. Houston broke into the Top 25 rankings for the first time since 1993.

The Cougars finished second nationally in turnover margin and averaged more steals than any previous UH team, including Phi Slama Jama. In fact, the Cougars led the nation in steals, a sign of a great defensive team that was fundamentally sound.

In 2006–07, Houston played at Rhode Island in the opener, and

Lafayette hit a buzzer beater in overtime for a 102–99 victory at Penders' old school. It was an exciting opener for a season that had its ups and downs. The Cougars played without star guard Lanny Smith in all but four games. "I called it the Murphy's Law year," Penders said of an 18–15 season. "We got hit by everything but a blimp."

Before the twelfth game of the season, a close 77–70 road loss at Kentucky, Smith decided not to play and rest his injured left toe. "My doctor told me when he evaluated it at the beginning of the season that he didn't think I could play this year," Smith said at the time. "I guess I was hard-headed and thought if I could work hard enough, then I could play. . . . It has been really hard to sit and watch my guys play, especially in a game like tonight when it was really close, and I thought I could help them. But, after the past couple of days, I feel that it is best for me and best for the team that I try to fully recover and come back strong next year."

Without Smith, Penders had to reshuffle his lineup, which included four double-figure scorers—Robert McKiver, Lafayette, Dion Dowell (a transfer from Texas), and Thorpe. "We had to have our leading scorer, Robert McKiver, play at the point in place of Smith which weakened us at two positions," Penders said. "We finished with a strong late-season run, but dropped a tough game to Memphis in the conference final."

Houston was 10–6 in C-USA, but didn't get a post-season bid for the only time in Penders' six seasons with the Cougars. Still, Penders' fifty-seven total victories his first three seasons were the most by any third-year Houston coach.

"Tom has improved the program very dramatically and I feel certain that will continue," Houston athletic director Dave Maggard said at the time. "We are on the right track. If you look at his record the last three years (57–39), it has been superb and it is only going to get better."

In the off-season, Penders hired his former Fordham guard Jerry Hobbie as an assistant coach to help with free throw shooting. And having Hobbie on the bench also re-emphasized Penders' work ethic and commitment to the program. "Basically, bottom line, Tom, even as an older coach: if you weren't a tough, hard-nosed type of kid, you would struggle playing for him," Hobbie said. "At the end of the day most of the guys on the floor wanted to win as badly as he did. And that is another strength of his coaching ability."

During Penders' first three seasons, the Cougars shot an average of 66 percent from the free throw line and were ninth in the league. With Hobbie on board, they were near or at the top of the league each year of Penders' last three seasons at UH. "I don't know if it is me," Hobbie said. "You are only as good as the guys you are working with."

Penders said emphatically, "Our foul shooting improved dramatically because of Jerry Hobbie."

In year number four at Houston, 2007–08, Penders had probably his best shot yet to make the NCAA Tournament—at least at the beginning of the season. Senior point guard Lanny Smith would be ready to play. Penders also had good off-season recruiting to add to an already strong nucleus entering the season. Besides Smith, Houston returned All-Conference USA guard McKiver, and starters forward Dion Dowell and guard Marcus Malone. Penders had added six-foot-eleven Marcus Cousin (a transfer from Seton Hall), six-foot-three Kelvin Lewis (a transfer from Auburn), and six-foot-one guard Zamal Nixon from Brooklyn, New York.

Houston had more home games (eighteen), including matchups with Kentucky and Arizona, than in his previous three seasons as the Cougars' coach.

An 83–69 blowout of Kentucky on ESPN at Hofheinz Pavilion right before Christmas provided some satisfaction. "Billy Gillispie (the Kentucky coach then) tried everything he could to back out of the game for at least three months," Penders said. Maggard held Kentucky to the return game unless the Wildcats wanted to pay a hefty financial penalty.

"We had an outstanding team despite not really getting the healthy Lanny Smith back for his senior season," Penders said. "This was a real disappointment for Lanny and our team. He contributed, but he had never really recovered from the foot injuries and he had lost a step or two. He was a hard-luck kid but never gave up. Nobody wanted it more than Lanny."

During the season, Houston had a ten-game winning streak but lost the opening game in the C-USA Tournament, 80–77, to UTEP on a controversial no-call. Houston lost heartbreakers at East Carolina, 84–83, and at UTEP, 87–81. Houston finished 11–5 and in third place in C-USA. The Cougars still managed to finish the season with a 24–10 record, the most victories at Houston since 1992.

"We were ranked sixth nationally in foul shooting (77 percent), but our best foul shooters had late-game lapses in both of those losses (to East Carolina and UTEP) and it cost us a ticket to March Madness," Penders said. "McIver averaged 23.6 points a game. We went to the new post-season College Basketball Invitational and made the semifinals before losing at Tulsa. We came up short (with the NCAAs) with a senior-dominated team."

HOUSTON COMES CLOSE TO NCAAS IN 2008-09

"We needed to reload with a great recruiting year, and that's exactly what we did," Penders said. "We were confident that we would do well because we were established winners who played very exciting basketball. We had a lot of points to replace along with valuable experience. We also had three very talented reserves returning in Kelvin Lewis (who had transferred from Auburn), Marcus Cousin (who had missed a month with a broken foot), and flashy combo guard Zamal Nixon. Anytime you lose five senior starters, though, it's hard to be overly optimistic.

"My personal expectations weren't very high, but we had solid people who found ways to win. I loved the confidence of our new recruits Aubrey Coleman, Qa'rraan Calhoun, and freshman point guard Desmond Wade. I thought they would mix well with the returning players. Marcus Cousin looked healthy and was solid at six foot eleven and 255 pounds. I knew we could establish an inside game with Marcus and the driving ability of Aubrey Coleman, a local player from Houston.

"Aubrey was the most explosive player I had ever recruited. He just needed to be coached up because he had played so little (previously). He was just oozing with talent and loved to play. Still, I knew we were in for some ups and downs trying to blend all the players. Memphis was the odds-on favorite to win the league, with only UTEP having the talent to challenge the Tigers. UAB and Tulsa also had solid teams."

Houston, picked no higher than seventh, took advantage of the lack of respect and thrived as an underdog. Tough defensively, the Cougars averaged more than eight steals a game. They had 137 blocks. And opponents shot just 41.4 percent against UH. In 2008–09, Houston took 441 fewer three-point shots than it did during the 2007–08 season. Houston went to the foul line 118 more times than its opponent did thanks to Aubrey Coleman who had 228 free-throw attempts. The Cougars had good wins against Western Kentucky and UMass in non-conference play.

"Aubrey Coleman and Kelvin Lewis developed into a great tandem," Penders said. "Aubrey scored thirty or more three different times and twenty-eight twice. Kelvin scored thirty or more twice. Aubrey did most of his damage in the paint and on the free-throw line. Kelvin did most of his damage beyond the three-point line." Houston went from a three-point shooting team to one that would emphasize Coleman's athletic ability.

"One of his strengths as a coach was his ability to make adjustments whether it was within the game or within the team he has in a given year," Hobbie said. "He sort of tweaks his philosophy every year. A lot of coaches stick with one system and they get stubborn. They try to win with it no matter what kind of talent they have. I think he has taken a step back a little bit. But one thing that has remained constant—he teaches the fundamentals. His fundamental belief in a thing such as footwork is one of the reasons he was so successful late in his career."

In 2008–09, Houston finished 21–12 overall and 10–6 in league play and lost to Memphis in the C-USA Tournament semifinals. But the key to the season may have been a controversial officials call during a non-conference game at Arizona in late January.

THE AUBREY COLEMAN AFFAIR

In this season, Coleman may be most remembered for an incident involving Arizona's six-foot-seven forward Chase Budinger. During a January 24 game in Tucson, Coleman was whistled for charging. After officials reviewed the play, he was slapped with a flagrant foul and ejected for stepping on Budinger. Not only did the Cougars miss Coleman during the final ten minutes of a 96–90 overtime loss to Arizona, they were without him the next game, a home loss to UTEP, after his one-game suspension by C-USA.

Put two more victories on Houston's record and the Cougars probably would have been in the 2009 NCAA Tournament instead of making a second-straight trip to the College Basketball Invitational.

Penders staunchly supported his first-year player, who wrote a letter and made a public apology to Budinger after the incident. Penders said Coleman was looking ahead at the official making the call and was trying to step over Budinger. Penders also said Coleman did not step on Budinger's face because the mark was actually left on Budinger's shoulder.

"I never meant to step on him," Coleman said later. "I have never been in an incident like this before, and I have nothing but respect for him as a great player. I love the game too much to do something like that intentionally."

"It tore my heart out," Penders said. "I know he never really would do anything like that. Even in practice situations where somebody has clobbered him, he never reacts."

Coleman put the incident behind him and was named C-USA Player of the Week when he returned from the Budinger incident. But Penders was unhappy that C-USA commissioner Britton Banowsky suspended Coleman.

"The ejection (and later suspension) possibly cost our school an NCAA Tournament bid because Arizona was one of the last schools admitted into the tournament (2009) and if we had beaten them on their home court, it might have been us that had gotten in," Penders said. "We would have had twenty-two wins, instead of twenty-one. And then we lose to UTEP (the next game at home when Coleman was suspended) and he was clearly the star of the game when we beat them out there."

C-USA officials said they were reacting to what was called in the game. "If there is an act of flagrant misconduct, there will be a minimum one-game suspension or more determined by the commissioner," said Chris Woolard, C-USA associate commissioner for sports services. "He could have suspended him four games. A flagrant foul was called."

"Banowsky never talked to me about (Coleman)," Penders said. "Our athletic director and president thought he was innocent. But after a few days of getting ugly emails, Britton decided to suspend him for a game. I thought he should have interviewed Aubrey and looked at the film and maybe even have flown down to Houston or have had Aubrey fly up (to Dallas) and explain what happened. I had to accept Britton's decision and move on. I am sure it was a difficult decision for him to make, too."

After sitting out Houston's home loss to UTEP, Coleman came out and scored thirty-five at Memphis. The UH basketball office was getting racist phone calls directed at Coleman from places other than Houston.

"Only a strong kid like Aubrey could have survived that. In the very next game after the suspension he played against Memphis and scored thirty-five points," Penders said. "There were some signs and then booing when he touched the ball, but it just made him play better. When they figured out Aubrey was not going to be affected by this they stopped. I told Aubrey if you are going to let them get to you—you know in your heart it wasn't intentional—but if you show weakness, people, except your family and friends, are going to get down on you. In reality, there are people who like to see people fail. There is even a word for that, *schadenfreude*, which means delight in another's misfortune. Sad, but true."

Penders said that Coleman should have been the C-USA Player of the Year during the 2008–09 season. "He is the best player in C-USA, and there are some really good players in the league," Penders said. "He really does more for his team. And he closes out games. He reminds me of a young Steve Francis (who played at Maryland and was a nine-year NBA player) or Ray Williams who played at Minnesota and later for the New York Knicks. He has a strong mid-range game and can take it to the basket."

And the best thing about it, Penders would have him for one more season in 2009–10.

THE MEMPHIS FACTOR

Part of the problem Houston had making the NCAA Tournament at-large was Memphis' great domination of the C-USA under Coach John Calipari. The perception was that the Tigers were so much better than any other team, the rest of the C-USA teams were not NCAA Tournament worthy. Over a four-year period from 2006 to 2009, only the University of Alabama at Birmingham in 2006 had made the NCAA Tournament as an at-large C-USA team, other than regular-season and tournament champion Memphis.

"They were undefeated in C-USA to boot," Penders said of the Tigers. "We knew only Memphis was going to the NCAA unless somebody pulled off a monumental upset at Memphis in the friendly confines of Fed Ex Forum during the league tournament. It's hard to beat a great team on their floor with 20,000 fans cheering them on. The referees might as well have been wearing blue and white. It was like the Christians trying to beat the lions in Rome. It wasn't going to happen.

"In 2005–06 they (the NCAA) ignored that we beat LSU (which wound up in the Final Four) and Arizona in the same week. And we played Memphis to the wire. UAB loses on a controversial call to Memphis. Some of us were worthy of an NCAA bid, but Memphis spends maybe five times as much as the other schools in C-USA. They put a lot of money into basketball. It is Memphis, Memphis, Memphis. And then everybody else gets ignored. And it was a league decision to run the tournament every year in Memphis because Memphis will sell it out."

C-USA has been able to clear $1 million in Memphis, so that is the threshold bidding cities needed to meet starting in 2005 when Memphis hosted the first of five straight C-USA post-season tournaments. Part of the problem was that no C-USA city stepped up to the plate and knocked Memphis out of the box until Tulsa did it in 2010. For the 2011 Tournament, El Paso has met the financial standard and will host the tournament.

"To C-USA athletic directors it was important to experience other cities and markets," Woolard from C-USA said. "Finally other markets stepped up and put in great bids to host the championship. They also wanted to pick a market where the home fans are supportive of the team. Tulsa was a viable option. El Paso was a viable option."

C-USA athletic directors want the arenas to be full and "the atmosphere to look good on national television," Woolard said. "Whether it is in East Carolina, El Paso, or Central Florida, the way the attendance stays robust is when the home team advances. That is who we are."

With John Calipari leaving for Kentucky in the spring of 2009, the aura of invincibility surrounding the Memphis program had somewhat dissipated. Josh Pastner, then thirty-two, became the Tigers' head coach in 2009–10. Tigers' guard Derrick Rose was off to the NBA. Memphis still had good players, but several teams in the league believed they had a shot at beating the Tigers. And with the C-USA Post-Season Tournament moving to Tulsa in 2010, Memphis no longer had a home-court advantage.

Pastner, a former walk-on at Arizona, was an assistant coach there before moving to the Memphis staff as the third assistant prior to the 2008–09 season. For years, his father, Hal Pastner, had run AAU tournaments in Las Vegas and Houston while sponsoring the best AAU team in Houston.

"Josh is a bright, young coach, but I know how important experience is and how much coaching means in college basketball," Penders said. "He has a genuine, friendly personality, but I doubt if Josh would have been hired at Memphis without the AAU connections that his father provided. Hal knows everybody in the country who is involved with AAU basketball. My attitude toward Josh is that he will have to prove himself as a college coach regardless of who his father is. It's a dog-eat-dog business and many of Josh's peers will want to make it very tough on him. If he's good, he'll survive and advance. But following John Calipari's success, Memphis is a tough job.

"Many still favored Memphis heading into the 2009–10 season. I was not afraid of Memphis. More importantly, my players thought we were better than Memphis."

REDEMPTION
IN HOUSTON

"'Dead Man Walking' was an expression yelled by the prison guards to alert the other guards that a prisoner on Death Row was coming through, and since he had nothing to lose he might do something crazy. As motivation for my team, I used the expression to say they had nothing to lose—to let go of the fear and just let it all hang out."

—Tom Penders, referring to his 2010 Houston team as "Dead Men Walking" to motivate them to win the 2010 Conference USA Post-Season Tournament

With Tom Penders orchestrating one of his best seasons coaching during his thirty-six-year college career, the 2009–10 Houston Cougars stayed together through ups and downs and qualified for UH's first NCAA Tournament since 1992.

By winning the 2010 Conference USA Tournament with four victories in four days, the Cougars put an exclamation point on a season that was initially characterized by injuries and sickness, free-throw shooting problems by their star player, and an average regular-season conference record.

In the end, working through those problems and losses only made the team stronger. The resulting championship and NCAA berth served as a springboard for Penders to end his tenure at UH after six seasons.

The sixty-four-year-old Penders became only the eighth coach in NCAA Division I Men's Basketball Tournament history to take four different schools (Houston, Rhode Island, Texas, and George Washington) to the Big Dance. That was just another footnote to a season to remember.

"We became closer than any team that I could remember," Penders said. "I can truly say that I had a blast being part of it all. This is exactly how it was back in 1971–72 when I started. And I soaked it all in and enjoyed the transformation. They gave me every ounce that they had.

"All I could say was that I have never been prouder of any team that I had coached. They would go down as the team that brought the University of Houston back from obscurity to the NCAA Tournament. They set the bar for future teams at the University of Houston."

The 2009–10 Cougars won the school's first C-USA Basketball Tournament championship. They became Penders' first team to win a tournament, by beating four teams in four days. Houston was the first C-USA team to win four games in four days in the tournament since Saint Louis University did it in 2000. By advancing to the C-USA title game, Penders became the first coach at UH to win at least eighteen games in six straight seasons.

Long before the C-USA post-season tournament, Penders declared that the non-conference part of the season was just a warm-up. The conference schedule was going to be all about positioning and building team confidence for the C-USA Post-Season Tournament and a grand finale at UH.

Although Penders had three seasons left on his contract, he just wanted to win the league playoffs and take Houston back to the NCAAs after an eighteen-year absence. Then he could take a break or a permanent vacation from college coaching. He had turned six-ty-four back in May and had never wanted to be like Larry Brown or Jim Calhoun and coach into elder statesmanship.

"I worked to live, not lived to work," Penders said. "I could coach forever, but I had no reason to want to put up with all of the other nonsense that permeated the sport of college basketball. I wanted to write books, travel the world, and perhaps do something in televi-sion or radio. When you coach at the college level there is no such thing as a day off even if you try to take some time to get away.

"It seems like every time you try to get away you get that 2 a.m. phone call that your star player is in the hospital, or he flunked his summer school class. I can't even count the times that family trips have been broken up because of issues like these. I've always tried to involve my family in my job. And they've basically loved the experi-ence. But nobody loves it when you just can't get away for a peaceful family trip without the fear of it being ruined by a cell phone call.

"I had a bunch of championship rings, but I was not leaving Houston until I earned one here. I never coached because of the money, and I didn't need the money anymore. This was about pride. Only Memphis had won a C-USA basketball championship since the 2004–05 season. No other school had come close. But we were poised to change all of that in 2010."

With guards Aubrey Coleman, Kelvin Lewis, Desmond Wade, and Zamal Nixon returning for 2009–10 season, the Cougars' back-court was set. On paper, Houston's new recruits would beef up the front line: freshman power forward Kendrick Washington (six foot seven, 270 pounds), who reminded people of Glenn "Big Baby" Davis, who played at LSU and is now with the Boston Celtics; juco forward Maurice McNeil (six foot nine, 215 pounds), a great re-bounder who ran like a sprinter and had a wing span of a guy who was five inches taller.

The additions of junior college transfer Adam Brown, a six-foot-four perimeter shooter, would give Coleman and Lewis added support. Freshman recruit Kirk Van Slyke, a lanky six-foot-nine forward, was a good outside shooter, even behind the three-point line.

Houston's individual players, however, had travails leading up to and during the season. Washington had to overcome two broken legs. Nixon played through a bout of mononucleosis. Coleman showed up in every game despite a painful deep thigh bruise. Maurice McNeil overcame worrying about his mother's diabetic condition and surgery. Even Van Slyke had health problems from a strep infection during the post-season.

"We were beat up a little bit, and guys were still trying to figure out their roles," Houston assistant coach Jerry Hobbie said. "It was hard to get over the hurdle. It seemed like there was one thing after another." But great coaches seem to have a way with hurdles.

Houston's third game of the season in the first round of the Great Alaska Shootout was a barometer of what the Cougars could achieve. The Sooners had a big front line and a lot of talent, but Houston's guards eventually wore them down. Oklahoma was up big with about six minutes left in the first half, but Penders called time out and put a four-guard lineup on the floor and went to a 2–1–2 press. Oklahoma got caught up in a track meet and committed a bunch of turnovers. Houston won going away, 100–93. Coleman scored twenty-eight and Lewis added twenty-seven. They would be the Cougars' big scoring guns all season.

Shortly thereafter, Houston coaches had to fix Coleman's surprisingly poor free-throw shooting if the team was to have success in close games. He was having problems with his mechanics and his confidence level was low in December and early January. Hobbie, a former player of Penders at Fordham who shot 87.5 percent from the line in college, worked with Coleman. He was knocking them down with a great stroke in practice.

Penders also had a close friend, Fran Pirozzolo, the famous sport psychologist, work with Aubrey. Pirozzolo owns four World Series rings after working from 1996 to 2002 with the New York Yankees. Pirozzolo also has been working with the 2010 American League champion Texas Rangers. "Fran was sure that he could help Aubrey out, but he said it might take a few games before Aubrey really bought in," Penders said. "I was just hoping that it would not cost us too many more games because Aubrey was one of our best foul shooters and he was always getting fouled. Plus, he was the top scorer in the country all season long."

Houston stood at 7–3 at the Christmas break. But in three games around the Christmas break Coleman had the yips at the free-throw line. UH lost all three games when he made five of eleven against Mississippi State; one of six against Louisiana Tech; and six for twelve against University of Texas–San Antonio. In the 70–64 loss to Mississippi State right before Christmas, Coleman missed four of five late and the Bulldogs scored the final six points to win.

On January 3, Coleman had only two free throw attempts, making one, at Iowa State in UH's 82–75 double overtime loss that completed a three-game losing streak. Houston generally outplayed the Cyclones, but Iowa State shot thirty-one foul shots to the Cougars' twelve. UH won the battle of the boards (49–45) and actually made four more field goals than the Cyclones.

"Our players were extremely upset, as was I," Penders said of the foul-shooting discrepancy. "I had a long talk with the team when we got back to the hotel because we were about to travel back to Houston and play Rice on Wednesday night on their home court. I told them that if we played this hard on Wednesday night we would blow Rice right out of their gym. I was feeling like we were coming together."

That's exactly what happened in an 83–66 Cougars victory over Rice. The injured Washington finally showed a glimpse of what he could do. In twenty-two minutes, he scored seven points and grabbed five rebounds. Coleman had twenty-two points on nine-for-fourteen shooting but again struggled from the line (three for eight). But from that point on, Coleman found his stroke at the line with determined work. The following game, he made fourteen of fifteen free throws and away he went.

"He was a great soldier," Hobbie said. "He was a great teammate. He came to work every day and did extra work. He worked hard on improving. Whatever it was going to take to get better, he was going to do it. He was very coachable."

Two other notable games occurred in January.

Houston beat UTEP, 75–65, a team that would be ranked in the Top 25 and finish the C-USA regular season with a 15–1 league mark. In a game at Memphis, which was tied at half 39–39, the Tigers exploded from the three-point line in the second half and scored fifty-three points. Houston lost, 92–77, which would be the Cougars' biggest margin of defeat all season.

Penders felt good about the later rematch with Memphis because the Tigers seemed soft on defense and on the boards. "That was another great thing about this 'special team'; we hung close or won every single game all year except for this loss at Memphis. Even their young coach, Josh Pastner, called it their best performance. I was very confident that we would win the payback game in Houston. The Tigers seemed to have the aforementioned issues, and they openly sulked throughout the game."

Before UH's return match with UTEP in El Paso in early February, Nixon had been complaining about feeling weak and had flu-like symptoms on and off: mono. He was able to play only eleven minutes and the Cougars lost a low-scoring physical battle at UTEP, 65–58, in which Coleman suffered a thigh bruise late in the game. Zamal always had played well against UTEP, and Houston missed his ability to attack the basket and knock down an open three-point shot.

With Nixon and Coleman still hobbled and their minutes limited, Houston lost the next game, a 59–57 decision to Southern Mississippi at Hofheinz on a tip-in basket as the buzzer sounded. It was the low point of the season.

"Afterward, I told the team that we were ready for the climb," Penders said. "We were about to become dangerous. We were 'Dead Men Walking.' I told them that this loss would mean absolutely nothing at the end of the season. There was only one way for us to get to the NCAA Tournament, and that would be winning the C-USA Tournament and receiving the league's automatic berth.

"I also told them that we were going to scale down the length of our practices to one hour, and we were going to have fun and get healthy for the championship run. I told them that I was saving all of my bullets for 'The Run,' and I knew that when we were healthy we were the best team in this league."

Penders would reveal the history of "Dead Man Walking" to UH players before the C-USA Tournament. Meanwhile, despite hovering at .500 with just an 11–11 record, Houston was loose and confident going to Western Kentucky. The Hilltoppers came out red hot and led by seven at the half, but Penders believed the team bonded in the second half for the stretch run of the season by winning a tough road game.

In the locker room, Penders told his players they were going to ruin WKU's "White Out Night" celebration that the school had promoted for the game against Houston. Mo McNeil and Washington played great, combining for eighteen points and fourteen rebounds. Coleman, despite his thigh injury, scored twenty-nine points and grabbed eleven rebounds. He was absolutely amazing in the final twenty minutes when Houston came back to win, 74–72.

Then, Houston played Memphis in Houston. It was a game Penders had waited for since their 92–77 loss to Memphis a month earlier.

Because Memphis coach Josh Pastner was from Houston, he had a lot of followers, media, and fans at Hofheinz Pavilion. Penders was tired of hearing that Pastner should have been hired at age twenty-six as the Houston basketball coach instead of him. There was no way Penders was going to let Pastner win this game.

Houston came out blazing and ran to a 43–28 halftime lead before cruising to an easy 92–75 win. It evened Penders' record against Pastner as a head coach at 1–1.

"The only thing I was disappointed in is the fact that we had to leave the floor for halftime," Penders said. "Josh was more than furious after the game, but he did shake hands and said, 'nice game.' His comments to the media after the game mentioned nothing about Houston, but a lot about his team's lack of effort and focus. I have lost many games, but I have always credited the winning team publicly. He'll learn about these things. Coaches and opponents have long and accurate memories."

After splitting games against SMU and Rice, Houston ended the regular season with a tough 79–76 loss to Tulane in New Orleans and finished with a 7–9 conference record. It would be the only losing conference mark during the Penders era at UH. But the best was yet to come.

The seventh-seeded Cougars learned shortly after the game that they would be playing tenth-seeded East Carolina in the C-USA Post-Season Tournament's first game.

"I think guys started to believe down the stretch," Hobbie said. "We hit a few roadblocks. We lost at Tulane. But I never thought our guys stopped believing.

"I remember Kelvin Lewis saying towards the end of the year, 'Hey, we are going to win this thing.' Kelvin, you looked at him, you believed in him. You look at what Kelvin did, he was the MVP of the C-USA Tournament. He felt he was slighted that he was pre-season first-team all-league and then did not get anything in the regular season. I think he took it upon his shoulders. He had that resolve and that belief that we could be something special. And Aubrey said the same thing. So when you have arguably two of the best guards in the league who are seniors who really do believe—that was instrumental in us winning the thing."

Before the Cougars played their first C-USA Tournament game, Penders gave the players a fax from the highly popular Jim Perry, who had been a co-captain with Otis Birdsong on the 1976–77 Houston team and an assistant coach for the great Guy V. Lewis. Perry, who lives in Detroit but had tickets to every UH game, sent numerous faxes to the UH team all season long. He predicted that Houston would win this tournament, and he wrote the team a motivational message reminding them about trust and to keep playing with the same effort. Penders called him UH's spiritual assistant coach because the players loved his faxes throughout the season.

"I finally told the team what 'Dead Man Walking' meant," Penders said. "It meant that we were about to die, but that meant that we would also become a fearless hunter that nobody would want to mess with. I told them that when I was growing up, I had to literally fight my way home until I earned the fear or respect of the bullies that I had to encounter along the way."

In the first round of the C-USA Post-Season Tournament at the BOK Center in Tulsa, Oklahoma, Houston cruised to a 93–80 win over East Carolina and conserved energy. Penders was able to substitute liberally throughout the game, stuck to a game plan, and showed Memphis little of anything they might face from UH in the quarterfinals.

"I don't think anybody realizes how good a coach Tom Penders is," said East Carolina coach Mack McCarthy. "His kids believe in themselves and what he's doing. They don't have all the pieces. But they have some nice pieces. They have small men who can step out and shoot the ball, big men who can run the floor and guard pretty good for their size. And, of course, Lewis and Coleman are really incredible. We had Coleman guarded a few times. And you can guard him, and he still makes shots."

In the next round, Penders believed that the Cougars had all the confidence to beat Memphis again. They merely needed to shut down the Tigers' three-point shooting to have a chance to win in the C-USA Tournament quarterfinals. He also felt Memphis might be a little tight because the Tigers needed to win this game to make the NCAA Tournament as an at-large entry. Memphis had not lost since UH beat the Tigers by seventeen on February 24, their worst C-USA loss since 2003.

Memphis struggled to go three for twelve from beyond the arc. UH's Desmond Wade was again flawless with six assists and no turnovers. And UH's defense was solid against a very talented Memphis team.

With fifteen seconds left Memphis had gone up by one and called its last timeout. UH had plenty of time to set up a play whether the Tigers were in man or zone defense. Penders wanted Desmond Wade to blow the ball up the court and run the X2 play for Coleman, who took it hard to about ten feet. The X2 play involved a quick handoff to Aubrey Coleman and a high, immediate ball screen that opened a driving lane for him.

Coleman then made a beautiful pump fake and got both defenders off the floor. He stepped through them and banked in a great shot off the glass with five seconds remaining. UH won the game, 66–65, when Memphis committed a turnover with less than a second to play.

Two more wins to go. Southern Mississippi was next up in the semifinals.

It was a back-and-forth game. Houston led by only two points with less than five minutes to go. Maurice McNeil did a great job defensively on Southern Mississippi star Gary Flowers in the second half and came up huge on the offensive boards when the game was on the line. Coleman again was stellar: twenty-seven points and five rebounds and converted ten of twelve from the foul line. Houston had only six turnovers, an excellent total against Southern Mississippi's tough and sniping defense. It was an exhausting and hard-fought battle, but UH won, 74–66.

Houston had about fourteen hours before playing UTEP for the tournament championship. The C-USA regular-season champion Miners, ranked twenty-first and winners of sixteen straight games since the loss to Houston on January 13, had drilled host Tulsa in the earlier semifinal game.

"Aubrey was really hurting and could barely walk after the Southern Mississippi game," Penders said. "He drew a great charge but got kneed in the thigh where he already was suffering. We packed him in ice and prayed that he could run the next morning. Game time was set for 10:30 a.m. for the nationally televised event on CBS. We were going to wake the players at 8 a.m., eat some pancakes, bananas, and juice and tee it up for glory!"

UTEP raced out to an early nine-point lead. But great three-point shooting from Sean Coleman and Kelvin Lewis kept UH in the game. Lewis played with energy and confidence on both ends of the floor. Coleman had a rough first half, going one for eleven and would make only four of twenty shots for the game, but he was getting loose balls and giving UH a spark on defense. UH trailed by five points at the break. Penders had four time outs left and did not have to show his four-guard look in the opening half. Winning or losing, he wanted to wait until the ten-minute mark in the second half, at least, before he went small. It worked.

The second half was played exactly like the first half in that UTEP would push its lead to eight or nine points, and UH would close it down with big three-pointers. With about twelve minutes left, UTEP's star guard Randy Culpepper had a breakaway layup, but UH's Desmond Wade tracked Culpepper down and gave him a hard foul as he tried to dunk. It was a clean and good foul. This would turn out to be a key play because Culpepper jammed his wrist and would not score another basket the rest of the game.

Despite his shooting difficulties, Coleman played a super second half when he handed out six assists and made four steals. UH spread UTEP's big team out and used the dribble with its four guards to go past the Miners' size.

"I said I wasn't about to shoot us out of the game," Coleman said. "I'm going to find my teammates. They were on and I wasn't going to be selfish. I wanted to do the little things that I did when I first started playing. I was a hustle man. So that's what I did. I got rebounds, loose balls, hit the open guy. I got some layups and big steals, but everybody came through."

With 3:14 left UH worked the shot clock and Coleman penetrated to set up Lewis for an open twenty-two-footer that splashed for three and a two-point UH lead. The Houston bench erupted and the Cougars seemed to raise their intensity on defense the rest of the way. UTEP tied the score with a put back before UH came down and milked the clock again. This time Aubrey passed to Adam Brown who drained a three pointer. UH was in control and won the game 81–73.

"I think the team you saw those four games was the real us," Lewis said. "I think that the games in the past we were up and down. . . . Four or five of the newcomers were coming in and had to get adjusted to college basketball and learned how you can't take a night off. The team you saw in those four games was the true us and what we work on every day."

Lewis, who scored twenty-eight points in the title game, was named the C-USA Tournament's MVP. Coleman joined him on the All-Tournament team.

"I really thought we could do it," Hobbie said. "Basketball is a game of matchups. And if you look at it, we went 4–2 against Memphis and UTEP, who had the best records in the league. We struggled against the bottom-end teams. We could have beaten UTEP all three times. We had a big lead there and blew it. . . . Winning the tournament wasn't that big of an upset in my opinion because we didn't get blown out all year. . . . The most refreshing thing, it all came together at the right time."

The UH coaching staff and team finally let it all out during the post-game hysteria. Penders' son Tommy and his wife Jennifer had driven all through the night from Austin and were on the floor celebrating while UH was cutting down the nets. Many thoughts were going through Penders' mind: He came to Houston in 2004 to turn the program around, build a winning culture, and do it without scandal. Mission completed.

"This is the most satisfying way to get to the NCAA Tournament," said Penders, who joined coaching luminaries Eddie Sutton, Rick Pitino, Lefty Driesell, Lon Kruger, Tubby Smith, Jim Harrick, and John Beilein as the only people to take four different schools to the NCAA Division I Men's Basketball Tournament.

Penders' son, Tommy, now the head high school basketball coach at Clear Lake High School near Houston, hugged his father and said, "Dad, you can't top this here, and it's time to go." Penders agreed.

"It's funny how my son could read my mind, but he has been around me so long that I should have expected such a comment from him," Penders said. "He knows the business and he knows me. I love him to death and I am forever grateful that he could be here for this incredible moment. My wife Susie was also out there hugging her second family, our players, and we finally embraced and she said to me, 'Now you can go, your job is finished.'

"What an incredible way to finish a season. We won against all odds, and that could be said about my whole career. I am a very lucky person to survive all that I have survived and just as lucky to have a great family that has been through thirty-six seasons of roller coaster rides."

The University of Houston won the admiration of the nation, and even the U.S. Armed Forces had a chance to watch and listen to the game.

"By the time we got back to the hotel next to the arena, my phone and emails were jammed full, but the first two callers were an emotional and proud Jim Nantz (CBS announcer and UH alum) and his buddy Jim Perry," Penders said. "They both expressed that they had tears of joy going. It's so nice to know that you have friends and even nicer when they impulsively reach out in times of joy and sorrow. I too felt wonderful that I could help bring back some national respect and pride for our two most loyal Cougars who just happen to be the best people and friends that a person could ever ask for."

After arriving back from Tulsa, UH had a relaxing Sunday and got the team and invited guests to watch the CBS Selection Show in the Carl Lewis Auditorium, which is part of the building that houses the athletic offices. There was a real buzz of excitement in the air.

The first region that was announced was the Midwest and right at the beginning of the show Houston was matched up against the ACC Co-Champion Maryland, ranked twentieth in the country. The Terps were seeded fourth and Houston was seeded thirteenth.

The winner would play the victor of Michigan State–New Mexico State game. UH's bracket was called the toughest in the NCAA Tournament by most of the analysts and experts because Kansas, Ohio State, Georgetown, and Tennessee were in the region.

UH was scheduled play at 9:30 EST on Friday, so they would have an extra day to prepare, but they had to fly all the way to Spokane, Washington, for the game. Houston athletic director Mack Rhoades showed great support by inviting the families of the coaches to make the trip to Spokane. (You cannot invite the families of the players. Paying for any of their travel would be an NCAA violation.)

Except for forward Van Slyke, who appeared to have the flu and complained of feeling weak, UH's health situation was fine. Penders tried to keep other players away from Van Slyke as he slept on the flight to Spokane.

Oddly enough, both Penders and Maryland coach Gary Williams were tied for fifth in career victories among active coaches at 648 going into the game.

"Maryland would be a very difficult matchup for us because they were very good and soundly coached," Penders said. "Gary is a little older than me and not the kind of coach that would be unprepared or look past my team. We both knew what to expect from each other. And we had very similar backgrounds. I was the starting point guard at UConn from 1964 to 1967 while Gary was in a similar role at Maryland. It was a game between two 'old schoolers' who had survived for decades! He loved to play up-tempo, press and run. Sound familiar?"

Houston battled Maryland for forty minutes but lost 89–77 to end the season. The Cougars played very well but once again struggled at the foul line (twenty for thirty-two) while Maryland connected on twenty-one of twenty-five free-throw attempts. Houston attacked the basket and drew fouls but missed the front ends of three one-and-one attempts. Coleman, who scored twenty-six, was unstoppable until he got to the foul line where he missed six. Lewis had another great game with twenty-four points.

"We were all heartbroken in that it was our last game together, but there was a strong sense of accomplishment in our locker room," Penders said.

Houston athletic director Mack Rhoades and UH Chancellor Renu Khator supported the men's basketball program all year long in many areas. Penders believes Rhoades has a very bright future as an athletic director. But a day after he got back to Houston from the NCAA Tournament, Penders met with Rhoades and told him that he would resign his post as head basketball coach after six seasons to follow other interests.

Penders felt that he had accomplished all that he could, and it was time to move on. It was the only way to go out.

"When you take on a challenge like I did here in the spring of 2004 and you change the culture from expecting to lose to expecting to win within months, that's major," Penders said. "Winning a league championship to put your team into what has become the number one sporting event in the entire country is a tremendous feeling. It's what I was hired to do, and I did it. When you have reached your goals at any level, it is time to move on. The people that are hounding you with love will turn into a posse with one bad season. That's just the way it is in this world. But I wouldn't trade professions with anyone. I was so thankful to the University of Houston for giving me such a wonderful opportunity.

"When you are fifty, you tend to be in denial about everything, but something happens when you hit sixty and things speed up more and more. What the heck is retirement all about? My wife is more than ten years younger than me and we're not about to enter an assisted living complex. It's time for a new challenge, but before I consider that, I have a book or two to write and some traveling to do without a basketball team in tow.

"You never see coaches resign when they are on top in today's world. There's usually shame and a scandal attached or you simply could not get the job done. I'm very fortunate because I have always managed to bring a program to new and brighter heights before moving on. I have been a survivor and this was a special team that learned how to survive."

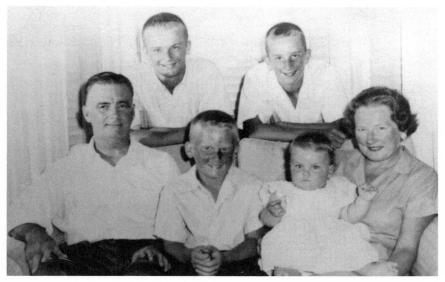

Tom Penders' family photo from 1958 in Stratford, Connecticut: Jim and Lillian Penders with their children, Jimmy, Tommy, Billy, and Kathy. (Penders family collection)

UConn's game at the old Madison Square Garden during Penders' sophomore season. Penders was an overtime scoring star in the Huskies' victory over Manhattan. (University of Connecticut photo)

March 1967 post-game celebration after UConn clinched the Yankee
Conference Championship. (Penders family collection)

Tommy Penders and Wes Bialosuknia, the best backcourt tandem of the 1960s.
They didn't keep track of assists back then, but Penders would have surely led the
country that year. (Penders family collection)

Tom (center) receives Unsung Hero Award from New England Basketball Writers Association from Bob Cousy (right). Tom's father, Jim, is at left. (*Willimantic Chronicle* Photo)

Tom (left) and brother Jim (right) take a break during a rain delay of a college game at Fenway Park in Boston (Harry Trask photo)

Waterbury Indians

AFFILIATED WITH CLEVELAND INDIANS
MEMBER OF CLASS AA EASTERN LEAGUE

203   757-1561
P. O. BOX 766
WATERBURY, CONN. 06720

March 7, 1969

Thomas V. Penders
93 Woolsley Ave.
Trumbull, Conn.

Dear Tom,

    We are sorry to hear that you have decided to leave
professional baseball, but wish you the best of luck at your
new job.

    If in the future you decide you would like to return to
Baseball, plea se feel free to contact me and I will be glad
to sit down and discuss this matter with you.

                              Yours very truly,

                              Bernard C. Durocher
                              President

Tom Penders and his first college team at Tufts. Far left (end) is Sam Bryant, assistant coach, the enforcer. (Penders family collection)

Tom at Tufts during a sideline moment with his team. (Penders family collection)

Tom Penders watches the action during his days at Columbia. (Penders family collection)

Tom and Susie wed in 1980 with Fordham University in the background. Kathy Flynn Muenz, maid of honor, and Assistant Coach Bobby Quinn, best man. (Penders family collection)

Fordham timeout during the Tom Penders' era. (Penders family collection)

Rose Hill Gym at Fordham, a NBC Television game vs. St. John's. Bucky Waters (red coat) and Merv Albert (in dark jacket). (Penders family collection)

Tom playing fast-pitch softball for Raybestos. (Penders family collection)

Fordham players Dave Roberson and David Maxwell celebrate with Coach
Penders after winning the MAAC Tournament championship in 1983.

Penders makes a point during Rhode Island's 1987–88 Cinderella season.
(Penders family collection)

NCAA press conference in 1988 after Rhode Island defeated Syracuse, 97–94.
(Penders family collection)

Friend Jimmy O'Brien and Susie Penders unmasked during Texas A&M game in 1991 when Tom was suspended for officiating comments the previous season. (Penders family collection)

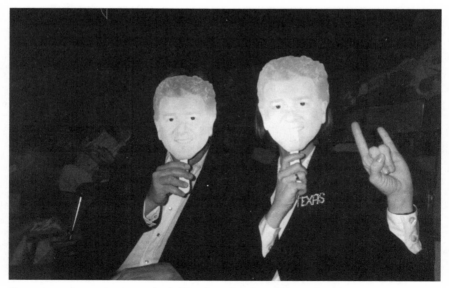

Same two, same game, masked. (Penders family collection)

Country-Western singer Willie Nelson and Tom on Willie's nine-hole golf course on Christmas Eve, 1990. (Penders family collection)

Tom Penders and former UT football coach Darrell Royal. (Penders family collection)

Tom Penders and former North Carolina basketball coach Dean Smith at a golf outing. (Penders family collection)

Tom Penders and Corby Robertson, UH supporter and former UT football player. (Penders family collection)

Texas playing at UConn during the 1993–94 season. (Penders family collection)

Penders' reacts to game action during his days at Texas. (Penders family collection)

Tom Penders celebrates one of many victories at Texas' Erwin Center. Daughter Karli (at left) also gives the Hook'em sign. (Penders family collection)

Tom Penders is working Westwood One Radio at Oklahoma State during his short hiatus from college basketball coaching in early 2000s. (Penders family collection)

Sideline view of Penders' coaching days at George Washington. Son Tommy (a GW assistant coach, in coat and tie) is at far left. (Penders family collection)

Tom Penders with his boyhood idol, Dodgers' pitcher Sandy Koufax. (Penders family collection)

Digger Phelps, ESPN commentator and former Notre Dame and Fordham coach, with Tom Penders at a gala. (Penders family collection)

Susie and Tom Penders at University of Texas black tie event. (Penders family collection)

Tom Penders cuts down the nets after Houston wins 2010 Conference USA Tournament. (Penders family collection)

PART II

THE ALPHABET OF COLLEGE BASKETBALL:

ADS, NABC, RPI, NCAA COACHING RECORDS, APR, AGENTS

ATHLETIC DIRECTORS (ADS)

My interview for the vacant Texas basketball job with Athletic Director DeLoss Dodds occurred on the afternoon before the 1988 NCAA title game in Kansas City, Missouri. I will never forget the four-hour interview in a suite at the Crown Center Hyatt because our meeting was interrupted two or three times by calls from Oklahoma basketball coach Billy Tubbs.

I remember DeLoss' wife, Mary Ann, coming into the suite and telling him that Billy was on the phone. Finally, DeLoss, somewhat frustrated by the intrusions, went to the phone and talked to Billy and wished him luck in the national game that night against Kansas at Kemper Arena. I thought to myself, "Here is the head coach at Oklahoma only hours before playing in the NCAA title game calling the athletic director at rival Texas and campaigning for the Longhorns head basketball job." I was kind of surprised he was not totally focused on the task at hand. Oklahoma lost to Danny Manning and the Jayhawks that night.

A couple days later, after a thorough vetting by DeLoss and his staff, I was hired as the new Texas coach. DeLoss dealt with me in this situation more than two decades ago in a highly professional manner, man-to-man. He and his staff did most of the legwork, then presented me to the committee and the University of Texas president for approval. But basically DeLoss hired me.

I honestly believe the reason DeLoss and I had a great working relationship for most of ten years was because *he* made the decision to hire me and supported that hire. We went to eight NCAA Tournaments in ten years and turned around the basketball program at UT. Certainly the relationship between a coach and an athletic director is crucial to the success or failure of a college basketball coach. Mutual trust and respect are absolutely essential in today's Internet and sports radio world. But the role of the athletic director has changed in some cases rather dramatically since I was hired at Texas in 1988.

Today, the roles of many athletic directors are as a fund-raiser first, administrator second. It's an arms race for big salaries and world-class facilities. Athletic directors often hire a coach with the help of a huge committee or a head-hunting "search firm." Some of these firms are headed by such people as Bob Beaudine, Bill Carr, and Chuck Neinas. This isn't a slam on these people. Athletic directors are sometimes forced to hire costly search firms because college presidents don't trust athletic directors to find the right coaches. In the past, the major responsibility for an athletic director was to hire great head coaches and then support those coaches so that they would have a chance to succeed. That has faded into the background. And who knows what criteria the search firm uses to match a coach with a school? In some cases coaches are hiring the search firms to do their bidding.

Some powerful schools still allow athletic directors to hire and fire coaches, but many athletic directors don't want that responsibility because they might end up getting fired along with the coach. If an athletic director can blame a bad coaching hire on a committee, search firm, or the president of the school, he or she might dodge the bullet.

I strongly believe that athletic directors should hire coaches and be held accountable for the success or failure of that coach. It would force an athletic director to support the head coach and make sure that the coach has the money and facilities to compete within his conference. If an athletic director can't raise money to keep up with the "Joneses" then that athletic director needs to go, unless the school makes it impossible to go out and raise the money.

I have worked with some great athletic directors over the years, and I think the ones I have had the best relationships with have been the ones who have been good communicators on a personal level. I've been lucky that most of my athletic directors have helped me be successful. Having a bad athletic director is like being in a bad marriage. Cut your losses, be civil, and step aside.

One man—Harry Arlanson, the athletic director at Tufts—hired me in 1971 at my first college job without a committee. A committee of many hired me at Columbia. My athletic director at Columbia had been a lacrosse coach at Hofstra. He knew nothing about basketball and cared only about football. I don't ever remember having a one-on-one meeting with him. I remember at Fordham, my next job, I was hired by an executive vice president.

An athletic director came along seven years after I was hired at

Fordham, and his main goal was to bring football back. I felt my future was elsewhere and jumped to Rhode Island. Athletic Director John Chuckran, who was a wonderful man and let me coach with his total support, hired me at Rhode Island. He also had a "rubber stamp" committee. Two years later, I went to Texas for ten years where DeLoss Dodds was a solid athletic director. We didn't always agree, but I know we had tremendous respect for each other. And the communication lines were usually open and still are today.

When I got the George Washington job in the spring of 1998, the athletic director there, a longtime friend whom I played high school and college basketball against, Jack Kvancz, made a trip down to Austin to convince me to take the job at GW. I coached there for three seasons. And in Houston, my most recent stop, in 2004, the process was much the same as when I got the Texas job. I interviewed with then-Houston athletic director Dave Maggard. On the initial call, I asked Dave if there was a committee. He said, "I am the committee." That's pretty much how it worked. Dave Maggard knew how to hire coaches.

Before my final season at UH, Mack Rhoades replaced Dave. Mack has a chance to be a superstar athletic director, and I'm sorry that I didn't work for him earlier in my career. He had a tremendous and very positive impact on our program. During our eight months together we won a Conference USA Post-Season Tournament championship. Every person in the program received a Super Bowl–type ring. We traveled very well, and our players received nothing but the best in food and equipment. Mack lets his coaches coach, and he created a great atmosphere in the department. It will be fun to watch him build something special at Houston.

Marquette coach Al McGuire retired after winning the 1977 NCAA title at the age of forty-seven. He was a brilliant coach and promoter but later said he hated dealing with an athletic director who communicated through memos. That would be emails in today's world. He couldn't understand why an administrator who had an office down the hall would bombard him with memos instead of verbalizing.

I believe athletic directors who rely on emails instead of personal face-to-face communication are just creating a paper trail and an atmosphere of distrust. Sometimes an athletic director or coach needs to use email to sum up a meeting, but otherwise it shows a personality flaw and outright recklessness. Some administrators rely on this method of communication on an everyday basis. Sometimes they copy people who work under the person receiving the email. Sooner or later those emails are all over the university. It's flat out suicidal, but people do it until they bury themselves in their own emails.

A smart athletic director keeps the emails short and infrequent and never criticizes anyone in email form. It's hard to keep things secret on a college campus, and emails can be circulated within seconds of receipt. There is no such thing as a confidential email, and I strongly urge coaches and athletic directors to pick up the phone or drop by the office instead of emailing.

Al McGuire was always ahead of the curve, and he was dead on when he talked about memos. A general rule is the less you put down on paper or on the computer, the easier your life and job will become.

Looking at old notes from coaching clinics I found some of Al McGuire's warnings for coaches in reading and rating their athletic directors. The following are some of Al's pearls of wisdom:

1. No athletic director should ever meet with your players or a player without your permission or without the head coach in attendance.

2. If you find out that one of your assistants has had private meetings with the athletic director, fire the assistant and look for job openings ASAP.

3. If your athletic director stops traveling on road trips, you need to look for a fire escape because you don't have his support.

4. An athletic director should never come near your locker room after a game unless you have invited him to do so. Your locker room is a private sanctuary for your players and coaches only.

5. If an athletic director tells the media he is going to evaluate your program after the season, get a new résumé and find the fire escape.

6. If your athletic director writes you memos instead of talking with you, gas up your car and buy a road map.

7. If your athletic director guts your budget without your input or approval you have lost his backing; he is setting you up to fail.

I have found out over the years that these pearls from Coach Al are incredibly accurate.

NABC

The National Association of Basketball Coaches (NABC) was started way back in 1927 to give coaches a voice in their sport. By joining the NABC and paying annual dues, coaches have been entitled to purchase tickets to the NCAA's Final Four and to participate in clinics, receptions, and award banquets.

NABC members include college basketball coaches from every level: Divisions I, II, III, NAIA, junior colleges, and high schools.

Coaches can still belong to the NABC even after retiring, being fired, or just moving into another livelihood. Dues are now close to one thousand dollars annually. I have been an active member since the 1970–71 season when I first became a college head coach at Tufts.

There are many things that the NABC tries to do and with the best of intentions. I just wish that the NABC would try to do more to help more coaches. Coaches need help in everything from legal advice, negotiating contracts, basic insurance coverage, and disability insurance. The NABC would be the perfect group to facilitate some of these things.

There are many ailing and suffering ex-coaches out there who need medical and financial help to survive. I hope that the NABC grows to become the organization that eventually does the things that our professional brothers have seemed to do for their former players and coaches. I'd like to see the NABC become more of a union than an association and provide the following assistance:

1. Legal help for a coach to fight a school after a questionable termination. Ohio State's Jim O'Brien is a case in point here. He eventually won his lawsuit. His compassionate act of helping a family and a young man during the war in Yugoslavia should have been applauded, not condemned as his athletic director did. Anyone who knows Jim O'Brien also knows that he is not a cheater.

2. A coach who has trouble paying his medical bills might be aided by insurance attached to every NABC membership.

3. Retired coaches, who are still paying their dues, may receive monetary relief from a fund established to help aging coaches through tough times.

4. Helping unemployed coaches find jobs, more than just a job board or how to interview. Former Arkansas coach Nolan Richardson, after his lawsuit against the school when he was fired, never did get another college job. There are a number of good coaches out there right now.

I know some of these ideas take money. Perhaps the NABC is working on some of these things. Those in charge are good people. I just hope that they continue to grow in numbers and in strength. When you look at the professional sports organizations and all that they are doing for the ex-players and coaches, I think you have models that could be duplicated at the college level.

The NABC elects officers every year, but they are basically too busy with their coaching duties to act as anything other than spokesmen and figureheads. Jim Haney, a former assistant, head coach, and conference commissioner, acts as the NABC executive director. Reggie Minton, the well-liked and respected former coach at Air Force, is the associate director. They work hard and were largely responsible for building the College Basketball Hall of Fame in Kansas City, Missouri. They ensure dues-paying coaches have tickets for the Final Four games each season—no small task. But some things have bothered me over the years with the tone they have taken toward some coaches who may have had rules violations involving the NCAA.

I remember attending a meeting in Indianapolis when they publicly scolded former Oklahoma and Indiana coach Kelvin Sampson, who happens to be a friend of mine. I was uncomfortable with the way they were handling the matter. Maybe they were embarrassed that Sampson, who was president of the NABC in 2003–04, had had a problem with making impermissible phone calls to recruits and was cited for NCAA rules violations at OU shortly after serving as president of the NABC. But sending out a public letter of censure and taking away his Final Four tickets seemed a little over the top. Even what happened at Indiana, when the NCAA cited him for what apparently were some inadvertent three-way phone calls, seems rather foggy to the mind. We are talking phone calls here. Any coach who really wants to violate this rule could go down to the local drug store and buy a throw-away phone. So it is hard to believe Sampson would intentionally break the rules at Indiana. I don't think the NABC should have publicly censored Kelvin Sampson. That's just my opinion. But I know that Jim Haney and Reggie Minton are good people.

Many years ago when Bob Knight was still at Indiana, he invited his friend, the late Bo Schembechler, who was the head football coach at Michigan, to speak at one of our summer NABC meetings. Bo gave an incredible speech and suggested that football and basketball coaches should join forces and create a stronger union. It all made tremendous sense. Bo had us so pumped up that we were ready to come out of the tunnel and kick ass. Sadly, nothing ever sprouted from that meeting, but I wish it had. Getting football and basketball coaches together would have created more of a union. We might have been able to get almost anything done, but it never happened.

THE RPI AND THE NCAA TOURNAMENT SELECTION COMMITTEE

Two of the biggest jokes in college basketball are the RPI and the Selection Committee. Let's address the RPI first. What the heck is it and how did it come to fruition?

The RPI is nothing but a compilation of statistics that allows the current powers to remain at the top. Teams from the power conferences seldom leave home to play tough non-league games. They have all of the money and they buy nine or ten victories each season to pad their records. Elite schools budget for guarantee games. The going rate is from $60,000 to $100,000.

Even at Houston, we were offered $100,000 to play at Syracuse (with their Big East officials and without a returning game to Houston), but a program is prostituting itself when it enters into a losing proposition such as that. At Houston, we had a budget of approximately $300,000 to offer several smaller schools to play us at Hofheinz Pavilion without Houston returning any games to those schools. Coaches at some of the smaller schools even joke about whether they are $60,000 or $100,000 "whores." They have to take these games to support their programs. Believe me, I know from my Columbia and Fordham days how it feels.

Aside from these guarantee games, the bigger schools might play two or three games on neutral courts with officials from their conferences protecting them. If this happened in football, people would be outraged. I know that some football programs play eight home games, but they usually pay heavily in the BCS Standings if they play *all* creampuffs.

The NCAA should put a limit on home games in college basketball or pass a rule where every school has to play at least six road games in its non-conference schedule. Road records are the only true measure of a team's toughness. No team should play more than seventeen home games during its entire season, regardless of its conference. The only exception to the seventeen–home game rule would be if a team had to play twenty or more league games. In that case the team should be allowed one more home game for every league game starting at number eighteen. A team should not be able to buy its way into the NCAA Tournament.

Teams should be given credit for playing road games, whether they win or lose. Right now only road victories are rewarded, not losses. There are too many schools out there that depend on road-game guarantees to carry their athletic programs. Many of these schools should not be playing at the Division I level. But if all teams had to play six or seven road games then even these smaller schools would have opportunities to play some strong non-league home games. Instead of playing thirteen road games and living off guarantee receipts, these schools could keep their students on campus once in awhile and the students would have a chance to pass a course.

The schools that play all these road games are also the schools that don't have money for academic support, so the student athletes have no chance to make decent grades when they are not in class. The coaches at these schools have no chance to survive; they have no chance to build a decent record and advance in their careers.

Five-seeded Butler in 2010 and eleven-seeded George Mason in 2006 advanced to the Final Four. But they can't get power teams to play them at home, obviously affecting their RPI and seeds. Schools such as Gonzaga, Xavier, Creighton, and Virginia Commonwealth over the years can beat almost anybody, but they have little chance to receive a high seed because nobody will play them at home or on the road.

I spent twenty-six years of my career at schools that had to go on the road because nobody would schedule us or we had to get guarantee dollars to keep our program afloat. I would estimate that I coached close to 60 percent of my 1,086 games away from home. I coached more college games than Lute Olson, Don Haskins, Hugh Durham, Adolph Rupp, and Marv Harshman. I guarantee you that none of those coaches played more than 50 percent of their games away from home. Willie Nelson's "On the Road Again" is the theme song for my lengthy career.

The Basketball Selection Committee is the most powerful committee in the NCAA, but how are the members chosen? It's a big secret. How many of these committee members even know the rules of the game? How many have coached or played the sport? There is just too much money at stake to have a group of people deciding which schools and leagues are going to make all of the money. The committee should be made up of people who have coached the game and have no affiliation with any school or conference. They should be former coaches who have coached at least fifteen years, and they should all be paid for their services. They should be held responsible and accountable for all of their selections. It should all be 100 percent transparent.

There should be minutes recorded, and every individual should have his own list of at-large selections. There should be a three-person sub-committee that evaluates the work of this group. The Selection Committee should be assigned by a czar-type person who works for and answers to the NCAA. This person today would be Greg Shaheen, who coordinates the committee for the NCAA. This would take the politics out of the selection process.

I am not accusing anybody of favoritism or cronyism, but the process is absurd when one considers that livelihoods and the existence of programs are at stake every March.

Millions of dollars are also being distributed at the whim of this committee. After the teams are picked every year, the committee's chairman faces the cameras and the faceless members usually slip through a rear exit and never have to explain what went on in the selection process. It's all a huge secret and nobody is held accountable. We ask politicians and CEOs to be held accountable in this day and age, but we demand no accountability from the most powerful committee in college sports. I repeat: I am not accusing any person or persons of shady practices, but there is no accountability as things stand today.

NCAA ON FORFEITS AND COACHING RECORDS

We all know that some coaches have been forced to vacate their entire seasons because of the use of ineligible players. But often it is not reflected in the records that stand beside their names in the school record books. Why not? How about the losses that innocent coaches suffered at the hands of those who used ineligible players or players who had signed with agents or accepted illegal benefits? The losing coaches can't subtract those losses from their records. There needs to be a national accounting—perhaps the NCAA should do it—to deal with all of this confusion and how schools calculate coaches' records. If the schools have the discretion to do what they want, they may not take away tainted victories.

It is crazy to say the school has to vacate its season and forfeit all of its games, in effect making the season's record 0–30, for example. Yet the coach at the same school still counts the illegal victories in his personal career won/loss record. The schools' and coaches' records should be in sync and dictated by the NCAA's findings. Take the victories away from the offending school and coach and add the victories back to their opponents' records, period.

GOOD APR DOESN'T MEAN
HIGH GRADUATION RATES

In the spring of 2006, the NCAA president, the late Myles Brand, spent a couple of days at the Conference USA meetings in Destin, Florida. Brand brought assistant Kevin Lennon along to help describe the new rules that were being enacted to improve the graduation rates for college athletes with a strong focus on college basketball.

Dr. Brand spoke for about forty-five minutes and fielded a few questions before leaving for a conference call. That left all of us with the personable and friendly Lennon who is humorous, engaging, and about as candid as anyone I've ever met. He is not an academic-type, but he is a very strong administrator in the NCAA hierarchy.

Equipped with various visual aids and formulas, Kevin was doing his best to explain the APR. But in short, I have a friend who is a graduate of MIT, and she can't explain it.

The APR is calculated by allocating points for eligibility and retention—the two factors that research identifies as the best indicators of graduation. Each player on a given roster earns a maximum of two points per term, one for being academically eligible and one for staying with the institution. A team's APR is the total points of a team's roster at a given time divided by the total points possible. Since this results in a decimal number, the CAP decided to multiply it by 1,000 for ease of reference. Thus, a raw APR score of .925 translates into the 925 that will become the standard terminology.
—Source NCAA

To cut to the chase: The APR, in my opinion, is a formula that will help the big-budget schools achieve high scores, but it will do very little to help graduation rates.

I have some very strong and accurate facts to back up my statement about the correlation of APR scores and graduation rates. On March 17, 2010, *USA Today* printed a chart on Page 11C of its sports section. On Page 1C of that same sports section, U.S. Secretary of Education Arne Duncan made a very strong statement about NCAA Division I Men's Basketball Tournament participants.

Secretary Duncan stated that if a school did not graduate 40 percent of its basketball players, then the school should not be eligible to participate in the NCAA Tournament. He stated that he did not have the authority to enforce his recommendation, but he would if he could. Naturally, I studied this chart on page 11C very closely. Houston would have qualified because the graduation rate was 42 percent. Secretary Duncan did not address the APR, because it was probably indecipherable for him as well. Houston had an APR of 900 according to the chart on page 11C. Some very reputable schools with higher APR scores, but very low graduation rates, jumped out at me. California–Berkeley had a very high APR score of 944 but a terrible graduation rate of 20 percent. Maryland had a respectable APR of 912 but had the lowest graduation rate in the entire field at 8 percent. Kentucky had an APR of 949 and a graduation rate of 31 percent.

The most surprising score to me was the University of Washington. Washington had an APR of 956 and an abysmally low graduation rate of 29 percent. The new president of the NCAA is Mark Emmert, who just left the University of Washington as the school's president. "YIKES!" is all that I can say about that one. Due diligence?

Everyone who has been in the business of coaching for more than ten years knows that a school president has more influence on a sport's graduation rate than any other person at a college, including the director of academic support, the athletic director, and even the provost. The president sets down all of the rules and doles out all of the funding to the athletic directors for academic support. Coaches have no input into the admission process at any school I have worked with except at Columbia, where I had some input through a rating scale that I gave prospective students.

How can an NCAA president rule over an APR system that has proven to be a failure at the university that he presided over? Brand and Lennon both insisted, back in May of 2006, that this APR formula would improve graduation rates. It's time to reevaluate this APR formula or severely tweak it, as Brand and Lennon insisted they would if weaknesses became evident. Well, I have just given serious and factual evidence that the APR is not a good indicator for graduation success at Tier I and other big-time schools. Georgia Tech is certainly a Tier I school with a respectable APR (914) and a subpar graduation rate of 38 percent.

If Secretary Duncan had power over the NCAA then Washington, California–Berkeley, Georgia Tech, Maryland, and Kentucky would have been dismissed from the 2010 NCAA Tournament. In the fall of 2010, Washington and Houston both were recalculated. Washington's graduation rate "soared" to 42 percent and the University of Houston's graduation rate improved to 50 percent. On October 28, 2010, the *Houston Chronicle* published a report on the graduation rates for basketball for the last four years in the state of Texas. TCU led the way with a 93 percent graduation rate. Houston finished in the middle of the pack with a 50 percent graduation rate. Big-time BCS schools like Texas Tech (44 percent), Texas (42 percent), and Baylor (38 percent) all had much higher APR scores than Houston but much lower graduation rates. These rates were for men's basketball only.

Rather than put you to sleep with mathematical equations, I will state that the APR is all about spending big money to keep players from transferring and staying eligible, but it has very little to do with graduation rates. Even though I am no longer working at the University of Houston, I contributed $20,000 to their academic support program in hopes of helping the student basketball players and the program's APR.

I think that the University of Houston really wants to keep improving its APR and to graduate all of its basketball players. The players have to go the extra mile, but the more money that is put into academic support the better their chance to graduate. If a school does not invest big money in its academic support program then it will drop below the minimum APR requirements, lose scholarships, and eventually be ruled ineligible to play in NCAA-sponsored tournaments, regardless of the school's graduation rate.

This will continue to be the case until the NCAA adjusts and tweaks this confusing formula. I was a pretty good student and strong at math, and I can't tell you why this formula is any indicator for improving graduation rates. Coaches all care dearly about their players graduating, but the universities and colleges have to make a strong financial commitment to make this happen. And it all starts and ends with the school's president. What the president wants will get done or a lot of athletic directors and academic support directors will be looking for new jobs. It's as simple as that.

AGENTS FOR COLLEGE FOOTBALL AND BASKETBALL PLAYERS

Should college or amateur athletes be able to have agents and lawyers without giving up their NCAA eligibility? Absolutely. And Big 12 Commissioner Dan Beebe agrees totally on this concept. Why not? Will it stop the cheaters from cheating? No, but we will stop making criminals out of the many college football and basketball players who already have agreements with agents.

What makes an agreement with an agent so wrong? How many thirteen-year-old golfers and tennis players have agents already? And many go on to play at the collegiate level. Is it because so many of these football and basketball players are minorities and come from extremely poor socio-economic backgrounds? Do you think that just maybe Tiger Woods or his father had an agent and a Nike deal before he enrolled at Stanford? How about Venus and Serena Williams when they were young teenagers? Come on; let's get our heads out of the sand.

The athletes and the sports would all be better off if the NCAA would allow young athletes and their parents or lawyers to arrange contracts with legally recognized sports agents. It would stop the absurd notion that all college athletes should be paid. The large majority of colleges and universities could not afford to do this because only a few turn a profit now. In basketball, as long as the agent is approved and registered with the NBA and the NCAA, let these agents sign whatever deals they want with these athletes.

Amateurism is a vague term. I played professional baseball back in 1968 and I was banned from playing in International Fast Pitch Softball events because I was considered a professional. In the early 1980s this ban was lifted, and all of a sudden I was an amateur and allowed to compete, but I missed four or five other opportunities between 1970 and 1980 because of a ridiculous rule. It is just a matter of time before athletes band together and litigate their case. And they will win out because this is America.

If a player cuts a deal with an agent before or during college and doesn't make it at the professional level, the agent loses the right to collect whatever funding he advanced to the player or student athlete, and all of this would be governed by the professional leagues and the NCAA. It's too simple not to create such a rule. It would not stop the cheaters from cheating altogether, but serious legal and NCAA penalties would apply for those who break these rules.

People will rob banks as long as there are banks, even if the banks are giving away free cash at $10,000 a clip on every Tuesday. Nothing stops greed, but this rule needs to be changed for the sake of transparency. If coaches know for sure that a player is only going to play in college for two years then he can prepare and recruit with certainty. It's a mess for everyone right now. The NCAA needs to get its head out of the dark, damp place where it is now resting.

AAU'S ROLE IN COLLEGE BASKETBALL

I could write an entire book on summer basketball and all the cor-
responding problems. The Amateur Athletic Union (AAU) in
some respects is a totally out-of-control organization that is running college basketball. I could say ruining college basketball, but
that would not be totally fair. There are some good AAU programs
where they actually coach and teach some fundamentals and team
concepts.

But some AAU programs are just all-star teams that rarely practice. A few are coached by people who shouldn't be allowed within
miles of the young people who play the sport. Over the years there
have been convicted felons, drug dealers, and pimps involved with
certain AAU programs because there are no rules, qualifications
needed, or checks and balances.

Years ago Little League Baseball passed a rule that all of its
coaches and administrators had to pass an extensive background
check. No such rule exists in AAU basketball. Parents and high
school coaches have a right to know the backgrounds of the people
who are coaching their children and players.

The whole system is totally out of whack. Players can play on ten different AAU teams in one summer if they want to do so. The big shoe companies—Adidas, Reebok, and Nike—pay the coaches and supply the players with countless shoes and gear. Teams travel to Las Vegas and Orlando and stay in four-star hotels. Who pays for this? Nobody knows, but anyone could make a good guess.

This whole situation creates unrealistic expectations. Even players who don't have double-figure averages for scoring or minutes played think that they are headed to the NBA. Their parents and AAU coaches have drummed that into their heads. It's not only unrealistic but ridiculous. It's easier to become a rocket scientist or a doctor than it is to become an NBA player.

The fundamentals of basketball, which used to be taught by the high school coach and honed by drills at summer camps, perhaps, have gone out the window. These kids just play game after game and never really improve their skills. Today, when a coach goes out during the summertime and sees a kid with good fundamentals, he gets excited. A kid like that is going to be over-recruited. Kids today are not taught how to shoot with proper mechanics. In the 1970s and 1980s, there were hundreds of great shooters in college basketball.

Sadly, if you don't play ball with these AAU characters they will do all that they can to ruin you as a head coach. By playing ball I'm talking about dead presidents (money). Many of the AAU coaches and owners won't give you the time of day unless you can help fund their programs and habits.

The city of Houston is a hotbed for AAU teams, and the people running many of the teams are looking for handouts. Rarely does a high school coach in the Houston area have a say in where a kid plays college basketball. They might be nice to you when you go over to watch a practice in the pre-season or watch a game. They usually will all say the same thing. "We are not really involved in the recruiting." So and so is 'handling' Bobby, so you have to call so and so."

When I was the head coach at the University of Houston, some of these AAU people would say to me, "Hey, we need Hofheinz Pavilion, as a place to practice." It is illegal to do it. But some coaches allow these teams to come in at night when nobody is there, and they practice in the facility. I was asked by about six different AAU teams, and I wouldn't allow it to happen. But I am not the security guard at Hofheinz, which was always accessible because a side door was always unlocked.

These AAU characters want to be hooked up with the important people at the shoe companies, and they want you to go through them in the recruiting process. They want you to pay for trips, hotels, food, and anything else that comes to mind. It goes on and on. This is where the boosters and alumni come into the picture. The coach usually doesn't have untraceable money to launder or hand over, but some boosters do. All of a sudden a coach is hooked up because he has a friend or a booster who wants the local team in the Final Four. Bingo, the deal is done, and now the booster and the AAU guy own the coach for life!

Many of the top programs in the country are involved with deals like this. It's like being in the Mafia because there is no way out. All they have to do is drop a dime to the NCAA or athletic director and the coach is history. Sometimes it's all done through an assistant who, strangely enough, used to be an AAU coach or sponsor. Or maybe, the sponsor of an AAU program is actually the father of an NCAA coach! How about that; what a coincidence! An assistant coach can move into a head job at a school because his dad or brother sponsors an AAU tournament or two or sponsors an elite-level AAU program.

The NCAA knows about such arrangements and conditions, but the rules haven't caught up with what's going on out there. Nothing is going to change until the NCAA goes after this AAU problem and nails the schools and coaches who are in bed with these people. Stevie Wonder can see what goes on.

I refused to affiliate myself or any school that I worked for with these people. No coach who has an ounce of integrity would allow himself to get involved with the slime element that exists in some of these AAU programs.

In the summer of 2007, I had a pair of odd visitors in my office. One was an agent and one was a head coach of a local AAU team in Houston. The agent had represented a player from my 2004–05 Houston team but was no longer his agent in the summer of 2007. The AAU coach was in his late thirties and had been a pretty good Division I player at a Southwest Conference school a few years ago. They were there to cut a deal that was not illegal but certainly on the shady side.

The agent didn't say much except that he hoped to be the agent of a local seven-foot prospect who had played for the AAU coach for the past few summers. The AAU coach did all the talking. He said that he could bring the seven footer to Houston if I would hire him as a full-time assistant coach on my staff. I told the two of them that their player would probably put his name in the NBA Draft after his first year and the AAU coach would be out on the street as soon as that happened.

I was very cordial in this meeting and wished them luck with all of this, and they weren't visibly upset when I turned them down. This past winter the NCAA passed a new rule that said if a school hires anyone closely associated with the prospect—an AAU coach, for instance—this person had to be a full-time recruiting counter (assistant coach) on the school's basketball staff. He couldn't be a strength coach, a video person, or a director of basketball operations. There was no way that I would ever hire an AAU coach unless I knew him extremely well. He certainly would have to coach, teach, and recruit. Once in a while this does happen and former Division I assistants end up coaching in AAU basketball and vice-versa.

There are some clean and well-meaning AAU groups out there (see end of chapter) that wouldn't think of meddling with the recruiting process or asking a college coach to help them get money. And those are the groups that have real coaches and want good players and good people involved with their teams.

Some AAU programs actually have an academic component involved where kids get tutored to help them prepare for the SAT. These quality programs are just as easy to recognize as the shady ones. The legitimate programs have reputable people at the top and usually some people who are teachers or educators who stick out like a horse in a dog pound.

But some AAU programs are deeply involved with agents or runners for agents and are usually hooked up with one of the shoe companies. These people also care about SAT scores, but they only arrange for someone else to take these tests for the prospect. Any student with a 75 average in a secondary school is unlikely to have taken his own SAT or ACT. It's ridiculous to think that a C student could score a thousand on his SAT unless he is prepping at Andover or Exeter. The colleges know this and so do the NCAA authorities. It takes some work to follow up to find out who is breaking the rules.

Colleges and universities often care most about winning, and the welfare of the student athlete is secondary. I'm all for giving disadvantaged youngsters a full scholarship. But how hard would it be to develop a standardized exam for English and math to be taken in front of faculty representatives? All scholarship student athletes must pass it before they are allowed to play. They should be kept off the courts until they can at least read at a twelfth-grade level and do basic math, at which time their athletic eligibility would start. Put an onus on the faculty at NCAA schools.

It is my opinion that phony SAT scores are flooding the system at a record rate. Let's end the hypocrisy and acknowledge that many of today's top athletes are not able to get the required minimum score. Let them be accepted conditionally, and give the university a chance to truly help this student athlete by tutoring him until he can meet the minimum standard of his fellow students. At that point, the four years of eligibility would kick in and the student would be better served to keep up with his class work. This would be another way of getting rid of the street people that offer phony SAT scores as well as thousands of dollars in name-brand athletic equipment to the top prospects in the country. Today's young prospects are not only being corrupted by this process, they are being cheated out of an opportunity to receive an education. It would be so easy to validate these phony test scores with photo IDs of the test taker or handwriting samples required at the time of the test. The current system is a farce.

I think the NCAA is beginning to wipe out the package deals and payoffs that are rampant in today's college hoops scene. The biggest problem today is that many athletic directors are encouraging coaches to hire AAU coaches, or friends and relatives of AAU coaches, so that they can land the top AAU players even if the players have never heard of an SAT score or know what ACT actually stands for. The ADs and university officials are in denial about the fraudulent scores.

A few years ago, Kansas State hired current NBA star Michael Beasley's AAU coach, Delonte Hill, as an assistant and reportedly paid him between $400,000 and $450,000 in annual compensation. He was one of the highest, if not *the* highest, paid assistants in college basketball. Similar, albeit less outlandish, deals are going on in college basketball today at several major programs. Does somebody have to wind up in the trunk of a car before this is cleaned up? This

AAU stuff is not isolated. Street agents, runners for agents, and the alumni are all back in bed again. An assistant wants the big payday, and he knows that if his school lands a few blue-chip recruits then he might be on his way to riches.

Except for a few rare cases, a head coach is not going to risk his whole career by getting involved with the alumni/agent alliance, but he knows damn well what type of person he can hire who will be more than willing to go that route. Head coaches who have been around can spot these assistant "coaches" from a mile away. These guys are usually jumping up and down during the television games to be noticed. The head coach would love to see these rogue assistants move on and land a head job at a lower level school, just to get away from them. These rogue assistants are a scandal waiting to happen. Reputable schools and athletic directors won't touch these people because their jobs will be on the line if it all blows up. The problem is that there is a new breed of athletic director who thinks that the head coach has to get married to the AAU characters to recruit.

This doesn't go on at Duke, Michigan State, Butler, or Gonzaga. But it does go on at many schools. People who think they have a handle on the landscape would be shocked to find out about some of these schools. Every time I hear about an athletic director hiring a coach and then hear the athletic director say, "Coach 'Jones' has great contacts with the AAU world," I get physically sick to my stomach. The athletic director has just hired a coach whom he expects to cheat, and he has just told the basketball world that anything goes until they get caught!

In July 2010, the National Association of Basketball Coaches (NABC) and the NCAA made it illegal to support the famous, or infamous, Pump brothers' summer extravaganza that has been held every summer for the last decade. Who knows how many hundreds of thousands of dollars have been raised since this event began, and the proceeds go to David and Dana Pump and their foundation.

The Pump brothers have funded AAU teams and tournaments for years in California. Schools, coaches, and athletic directors have been paying hundreds of dollars every summer to support this event for fear of being blacklisted by the Pump brothers in their efforts to recruit players who are involved in the brothers' AAU program. Before they created this event, the brothers were famous for having, or gathering, hundreds of Final Four tickets, which they used, gave away, or sold every spring. The less visible and wannabe head and assistant coaches were the people who gave or sold their tickets to Dave and Dana. The NABC takes away your right to buy Final Four tickets if you get caught selling your tickets, so I suppose they just gave the Pumps their tickets to stay out of trouble.

The Pumps have been extremely powerful people in the overall hoops scene. They are very friendly guys and they never try to intimidate anyone, but it's obvious to anybody with any street sense that if you play ball with the Pumps they will try to help you out.

The Pump brothers have also served as sort of middlemen when schools are searching for a coach. More than a few schools have hired coaches at the Pumps' behest. Talk about clout and power. I don't know how their selections have worked out for the different schools, but it's amazing that a couple of AAU people would be advising universities in their search for coaches—amazing stuff but not against NCAA rules. Being a four-decade head college coach I'll just say that the Pumps are amazing guys.

Dana saw me at the Final Four a few years ago and told me that he heard that I was begging Ben Howland for a game to commemorate the fortieth anniversary of the "Game of the Century" that was played in the Astrodome between Houston and UCLA on January 20, 1968. Dana asked me why in the heck I didn't call him to make it happen. I told Dana that I had no idea that he could make it happen. He laughed out loud and said he would talk to Ben.

I called Dana a week or so later and he said that he would make the game a reality. He was in Pauley Pavilion as we spoke. Well, he never called back. There is nothing illegal about talking to the Dana Pumps of the world, but perhaps the NCAA ought to think about limiting phone calls between AAU people and college coaches because AAU coaches and directors have more influence on recruiting than anyone, including the parents of prospects and the high school coaches. The NCAA is finally addressing some of the AAU issues, but about twenty years too late.

The Pump brothers are like the "Brady Bunch" compared to some of the clowns that control some of the best AAU programs in the country. I don't know for a fact that they have ever done anything illegal, but when an extremely passive group such as the NABC throws a ban on your biggest fund-raising event, they must suspect something. I never went to or supported their fund-raising event because I felt that they were pushing the envelope. But maybe they were just raising money for a charity. The NABC and the NCAA ruled that after the summer of 2010 attending or financially supporting this event would be against NCAA rules. I've always thought that supporting any AAU people or event was suspect and illegal.

My solution for limiting the influence that AAU coaches have in the recruiting process: Make it illegal for college coaches to attend AAU–sponsored events. They can run all the events that they want, but the coaches have to stay at home with their families and players. It would cut down on expenses for every school and allow coaches to stay on campus to supervise their players.

A majority of player problems seem to occur during the summer because the players know the coach is on the road. Such a move by the NCAA might not totally solve the AAU problem, but it would bring some power back to the high school coaches and take recruiting out of the hands of those running summer basketball.

The NCAA has nothing to lose by trying this out. But the organization can't seem to pull the trigger on this piece of legislation despite the fact that in October 2010 the Collegiate Commissioners Association voted 31–0 in favor of eliminating the summer evaluation period, which is when the big AAU events occur. That's amazing.

THREE AAU PROGRAMS THAT DO IT THE RIGHT WAY

1. The City Rocks, Albany, New York is directed by Jim Hart, a Wall Street broker and Fordham graduate. He is a father of three girls, with one enrolled at NYU and another at Syracuse. Hart does not recruit players, but numerous players from the state of New York participate in his program. Hart's program, which begins with players at age ten, has helped many young people develop basketball and academic skills. He enrolls some players in the Kaplan Program so that they have a better chance to score well on their SATs and ACTs. Hart also urges his young players to play Little League Baseball. Players must show academic improvement to remain in his program. Hart is an honest man who does not get involved with the recruiting process. He will try to help players find schools only if they are not being recruited. Hart is respected by all college coaches. He raises all of his funding for team travel by hosting tournaments and reaching into his own pocket. Over the past couple of years Nike has supplied some shoes and uniforms to help defray expenses, but Hart says he receives no money from Nike.

2. The New Jersey Roadrunners is directed by Sandy Pyonin, a legendary coach and individual trainer who has dedicated his life to helping young players from New Jersey develop their skills. He is a school teacher who spends all of his spare time coaching and training high school–level talent. Pyonin brings his team to a few tournaments every year and has won several national AAU events. He raises all of his funds for travel and expenses. He has been an AAU coach since the mid-1970s and takes pride in the fact that he has never steered a youngster to any school. He remains in touch with all of his former players. Some, like the Denver Nuggets' Al Harrington, have come back to help him financially. But he never solicits money from former players or shoe companies. Pyonin is involved with AAU basketball for all of the right reasons. There has never been an instance of scandal of any sort with his program. He is more famous in New Jersey as a trainer and coach than he is as an AAU director. I've seen him take fifteen-year-olds with no real skills and develop these players into Division I prospects. He is a rarity in AAU basketball because he can really teach and coach the game.

3. The Boston Amateur Basketball Club (BABC) is directed by legendary Leo Papile, who started this program in the 1970s. It exploded in the 1980s as Papile drove large groups of poor kids all over New England to play in weekend tournaments. In 1997, Papile was hired by the Boston Celtics and currently has a title of senior director of basketball operations with the NBA club. He took the job with one caveat: He would not give up his role as director of the BABC. Since Papile started the BABC thirty-three years ago, he has helped countless youngsters find college scholarships, but he has never jumped in the middle of an ongoing recruiting process. Less talented kids in the program often get scholarships because of his collegiate contacts. The BABC has won thirteen national AAU tournaments and seventy-eight New England–area championships. Former NBA players Patrick Ewing and Dana Barros have come through the BABC. Papile does not sell his players on making NBA rosters. He pushes education and counsels young people about the importance of getting their degrees.

CBS AND ESPN

oaches are always subject to criticism by the media, and I have had my share of it during my thirty-six-year head-coaching career in college basketball. One day you are a brilliant coach who can't recruit, and the next you find yourself recognized as one of the top recruiters in the game, but your Xs and Os may be lacking. I've learned to take it all with a grain of salt. I feel privileged to have worked among the best of the best on television. I worked at ESPN for two seasons earlier this decade and for ESPN2 during two Final Fours in the 1990s and learned a lot about these professionals. The people who put coaches and the sport under a microscope deserve a little evaluation and criticism of their own, and I am going to take this opportunity to turn the tables and shine a little light on my friends and colleagues who control the airwaves.

ESPN rival CBS has televised the NCAA Division I Men's Basketball Tournament since the 1982 season but only televises regular-season network games on weekends and focuses on a couple of conferences—the Southeastern Conference and the Big Ten. CBS recently expanded to the cable and dish networks with the CBS College Sports Network. CBS could become a serious challenger to

ESPN by just expanding and promoting the relatively new network because its telecasts are excellent.

CBS is first class in every facet. Led by play-by-play announcer Jim Nantz, the coverage always has a tight focus on the game at hand. Clark Kellogg is the network's top color analyst, and Greg Anthony is fast becoming one of the best in the business. Anthony obviously prepares hard, talks to the coaches, and tells people what's likely to happen before it happens. He also knows the players' strengths and weaknesses. Kellogg is an easy listen and does not take himself too seriously. He has the "nice guy" persona.

Verne Lundquist and Gus Johnson are also outstanding play-by-play announcers, but nobody compares to the velvet-voiced Nantz, a University of Houston graduate. Nantz just melts into the event and never overstates the action on the floor. All CBS play-by-play people know enough about the game, but they never step on the color commentators' toes.

Bill Raftery is the pinch hitter as a color commentator, and his friendly and self-deprecating humor usually wins the audience over. Because Raftery coached at Seton Hall, some feel he has an Eastern bias, but they said the same thing about Billy Packer (on CBS) and Dick Vitale (on ESPN) in regard to their relationships with the Atlantic Coast Conference. Raftery also brings warmth to the telecasts. It's like sitting with him in a bar listening to him. He is one of the all-time "good guys" in the college game, and I hope he never retires. Bill is a rare guy who can work every night of the week and easily slip right into the telecast.

Inside the CBS studio, Tim Brando and Seth Davis have a passion for the game that comes through during their halftime shows. Seth takes care of the latest rumors and is a very professional insider. Brando knows the game, the coaches, and the players throughout the country and prepares thoroughly.

CBS has done a great job with the NCAA Tournament and has been extremely creative with its coverage. In the opening rounds, fans have been able to watch their home teams in their local television markets. I'm not sure yet what role that TNT, starting with the expanded sixty-eight-team 2011 NCAA Tournament, will play. Its coverage of the NBA is tremendous. TNT (including TBS and truTV) can only add to the broad-based coverage and the excitement of March Madness, which has become the biggest and most interesting sporting event in the country. It is the most sought-after ticket and people are willing to pay any price to just get in the door. The television coverage of the event is phenomenal with round-the-clock interviews of coaches and players, replays of game highlights, analyses, predictions, coaching rumors. You have to be living under a rock not to get caught up in the excitement of March Madness.

The only criticism I have regarding CBS's regular-season coverage of college basketball lies with the programming. For the past two or three years CBS's weekend matchups have been woeful, particularly in the Big Ten. Somebody loves Michigan and Indiana there. And neither program has been on the radar for the past three years. Give us Michigan State, Wisconsin, Ohio State, Illinois, and even Minnesota, PLEASE! That is the only weakness I can find with CBS. If that is not fixed, CBS is going to lose some viewers to watch NASCAR in the early weekend hours on Saturday and Sunday. The halftime show with Brando and Davis saves the day. They are excellent, knowledgeable, and fun to watch.

My experience on the ESPN news set was invaluable. I had access to miles and miles of tapes of games and tons of research. The producers and directors afforded me great freedom to choose my own topics to explore and present to the public. It was great fun analyzing the college game from this vantage point. This allowed me a unique and up-close opportunity to observe, and now critique, the real world of sports television.

ESPN's in-studio announcers are exceptional and hard working, as are the people in the production area and behind the cameras. They have a research specialist named Howie Schwab who is an incredible fact machine. Howie was always there for the prime-time guys, who could bounce stuff off of him. His knowledge of sports information is better than Google's!

ESPN is extremely influential in college sports, with various levels of television contracts across all conferences. CBS may have the advantage with the SEC and Big Ten, but ESPN gets its pick of the rest of the games. They control who gets on TV and who gets the coveted time slots. There are only so many hours in a day, and this kind of exposure influences everything from recruiting to the teams selected for the final run of March Madness. Coaches' careers blossom or burst accordingly. ESPN is deeply involved in who gets where in the business of the sport. ESPN pays millions of dollars to certain conferences for the rights to televise their basketball games. ESPN's role has slowly changed over the years because it will shamelessly promote the BCS Conference schools and coaches with whom the network has multimillion-dollar contracts—the Big 12, Big Ten, ACC, SEC, and Big East. When the Pacific 10 becomes the Pacific 12 in the 2011–12 season, there are rumors that they will end their television deal with Fox Sports and sign a deal with the more powerful ESPN. Now ESPN gives the Pac 10 limited coverage, practically ignoring them all together. When and if the Pac 12 signs a deal with ESPN, America will finally hear about it. Who is the coach at Oregon? Washington State? Who plays point guard for California? Stanford? How about USC? Unless a person tunes into Fox Sports, he probably doesn't know the answers to those questions.

ESPN does not waste much time focusing on Butler, Gonzaga, or Xavier, and you can guess why. They aren't going to be guaranteed a lot of games, and their games will most likely be on the lower ratings weeknights. Exposure, exposure, exposure equals recruiting, recruiting, recruiting. It's as simple as that. Employees at ESPN play the game or they will not be on the air too long. So the "haves" continue to have all of the advantages provided by the big TV contracts and the "have-nots" struggle to stay alive, capturing some airtime if they are given a chance to play one of the big boys. And there lies another problem.

During the 2002–03 season, I was critical of the Big 12 for a timekeeper's error at Oklahoma that undoubtedly cost Texas Tech and Bob Knight an NCAA Tournament bid. The timekeeper sat on the clock and took at least five seconds away from a leading Texas Tech. That timekeeper allowed Oklahoma to score on a length-of-the-court play in the final seconds, tie the score, and send the game into over-time where the Sooners went on to win, 69–64. I felt strongly that the league should have stepped in and changed the outcome because it was obvious to me that the OU timekeeper was cheating Texas Tech.

Let's just say that the higher-ups at ESPN weren't too happy that I exposed Oklahoma's timekeeper, but I felt that the players at Texas Tech got cheated. I wasn't looking to become the next Digger Phelps, but I'm not one who backs away when I feel strongly about an issue. So I kept bringing that game up right through NCAA Tournament Selection Sunday. I was pretty tough on the Big 12 office for allowing such an injustice to go unpunished. Kevin Weiberg, the Big 12 commissioner at the time, was not sending me flowers.

During the NCAA Tournament later that season, I was doing color for Westwood One Radio when Commissioner Weiberg told me that I was wrong to criticize OU's timekeeper and the conference office. He also said that he had some strong ties to the people who ran ESPN. He went on to say that Big 12 officials questioned the timekeeper at OU and practically pulled off his fingernails, but the guy would not confess. It is humorous to me that they expected the timekeeper to admit that he had cheated during a nationally televised game. If the timekeeper owned up to cheating, he would have had to move to Alaska and OU would never have lived it down.

As a reporter who presented the facts, I'm glad that I exposed a very serious situation. But a lot of people would have ignored the whole episode to move up the ladder. I soon went back to coaching, and Commissioner Weiberg soon left for another job. Three jobs later, Weiberg is deputy commissioner of the Pacific 10 Conference.

I've seen more than most people about the television industry, and I do understand the business and "kiss ass" side of the television and coaching businesses. But I've never respected "kiss ass" people nor played that game in my life. I respect anyone who is honest and treats others respectfully. Having been brought up in the 1960s, I was taught to stand up for my beliefs. There is no compromise for the truth on my menu. In television and in the coaching profession there are those people who spend most of their time kissing ass and stabbing each other in the back.

Don't put me in that scorebook or even in the program. It was fun for me to see some of this go on at ESPN, but most of the people were upfront, honest, and extremely professional. I'm not going to waste space on whom I thought was kissing ass because that would be judgmental and unfair. Trust me, there is lip gloss all over the place at ESPN and most of it goes on with the part-time performers who have full-time jobs outside of ESPN. These people are praying for the chance to be among the main performers so that they can be one of the stars and quit their full-time jobs.

I didn't dislike anyone at ESPN, but some people working there would shove their loved ones under a bus just to get a few more minutes of airtime on *SportsCenter*. I observed this with a few of the football and baseball people as well, but the regular "on-air talent" were not a part of this group. We, and I emphasize we, had a lot of fun inside and outside the studio. It was so much fun to work with all of the guys and women who have to get in front of the camera year-round and perform at an amazing level every single day. Some were outrageously funny off air and always willing to help. I don't want to leave anybody out, but people like Neal Everett, Scott Van Pelt, and John Anderson could be on *Saturday Night Live*. Stuart Scott could be the next Bernie Mac if he chose to do so. While working with some of these guys it was hard to keep a straight face.

Okay, let's get down to the "Nitty Gritty" as they say on NCAA Tournament Selection Sunday. I've talked about the studio gang that spends twelve months a year in or near Bristol. Now let's talk about the analysts, play-by-play talent, and a few of the top announcers. Here we go:

Dick Vitale: One of the biggest icons in sports. The young crowd (students and kids) absolutely adore him. Nobody dares to emulate him because that person would get tossed off the air in three minutes. He has done more for the sport and coaches than anybody I've seen or met in my lifetime. He is one of the most sincere and genuine people I have had the privilege to meet. There will never be another Dick Vitale, and he's in the Basketball Hall of Fame! He's the best, baby! Don't try to copy this dude!

Dan Shulman: Maybe the only play-by-play announcer who can handle working with Vitale. He's ESPN's Jim Nantz. Pure class; no ego but knows how to present the game. Somehow he can do a game flawlessly working between Vitale and Raftery while keeping his sanity. Smooth delivery, great voice, and nothing phony in his act. If somebody is better than him at ESPN then I haven't seen that person. If Nantz quits at CBS, he's the only guy that could come close to filling his shoes.

Brad Nessler: A real pro who knows the game and has a great delivery. He's an easy listen and seems to know the game and when to let his color commentator talk. Could easily work at CBS, TNT, or step into any league in the country and do a great job without showing favoritism. He tells it like he sees it.

Dave O'Brien: Great delivery, voice, and knowledge of the game. He is excellent in baseball as well. He has a great future because he is always well prepared and doesn't favor any coach or team. Dave could end up as the next Vin Scully. Absolutely no flaws.

Brent Musburger: He's still the same after all these decades. He makes every event special and never tries to color commentate. He brings drama and excitement to every telecast. He's old school, one of a kind.

Sean McDonough: Basically sticks in the Big East. But he's a real pro. He's smooth and easy to listen to on the air. I get the feeling that, like Jim Nantz, he could be an announcer for any sport. He's a super baseball announcer in the mold of Dan Shulman. He never overstates or promotes—even his alma mater, Syracuse.

ESPN STUDIO AND COLOR ANALYSTS

Andy Katz: He's ESPN's Seth Davis. Has and keeps great contact with coaches all over the country. He's usually on the money with his inside scoops. Every year he gets better and better. While he is not a former player or coach, he does an excellent job of covering the behind-the-scenes news. He's also a superb writer who has a real passion for college hoops and the coaches. He writes for ESPN.com on a year-round basis. He's a good guy and worth every dime that he makes.

Doug Gottlieb: Tells it like it is and shows no conference bias. Was a great point guard at Oklahoma State and has a keen understanding of the game. He's always prepared and not afraid of controversy. Has an edge to his style, which I think is totally refreshing. Good game analyst and has a feel for what's going to unfold during a telecast. He's great in the studio and never hesitates to criticize. Knows about every team and coach in the country. He could easily be a college coach. Doug is also excellent on EPSN Radio.

Fran Fraschilla: I'd love to see him work more with the Nesslers and Shulmans of the business. Obviously, he wants to get back into college coaching because he never criticizes or second-guesses anybody. He is ESPN's expert on foreign basketball, which could be a curse to his career because very few people care about foreign hoops in the United States. If European basketball ever becomes part of ESPN's package (like soccer has) he'd be a go-to guy. If he makes up his mind to be a color analyst and forgets about another coaching opportunity while on air, he could be a lot better and he still might get another opportunity. He's a good guy, but he often goes overboard in his promotion of the Big 12 and their coaches. Just a little bouquet now and then would suffice. ESPN needs to allow him to work some Big East and SEC games to expand his horizon and knowledge of the national scene like Gottlieb. Steve Lavin did a good job of expanding every season and was ready for the climb at ESPN, but the crazy guy took the St. John's job.

Jay Bilas: Takes himself and his opinions far too seriously. I know he works hard and knows the game as a former player, but he goes over the top when he tries to demonstrate a play or gets too technical. He uses basketball terminology like hedging, showing, and sealing and never lets the audience know what he's talking about. He rarely gives credit to the mid-major teams, and when one of them makes the NCAA Tournament as an at-large entrant he throws a fit. You never heard him talk about George Mason or Butler until they made the Final Four. He works the Maui Classic every year with Raftery and Sean McDonough and tries to dominate the telecast with his academic "know it all" approach to basketball. McDonough and Raftery seem to pretend he's not there, but Bilas keeps on jumping in and often worries more about selling his opinion than describing and analyzing. Bilas rarely takes a stance on coaching scandals and other controversial topics that Gottlieb will grab by the throat. He needs to lighten up and let the game flow once in awhile. He seems to comment on every single play, which has to be annoying to the play-by-play guy. I wonder if he's given any thought to becoming a professor.

Jimmy Dykes: Prepares harder than anyone I've seen. Knows the game and is not afraid to predict what will happen. Was a player and assistant coach at Arkansas. Does not take himself too seriously and seems to have fun behind the mike. He's a good one.

Digger Phelps: What can I say about the former Fordham and Notre Dame coach? Nice ties, great highlight pens that match. I guess I'll just say that he's another icon. But he keeps Howie Schwab, ESPN's incredible research specialist, extremely busy. I love to see him go head-to-head with Bilas and Gottlieb because he comes close to losing it. He doesn't seem to agree with either one of them on anything. Digger Dame will always have a special place at ESPN, but I wish he would get an alternative line for "points in the paint." How about calling it "pay dirt" or "the red zone"? Digger has brought Zoot Suits back to the national scene. All he needs is a flower in his lapel that squirts water. Some night I predict that a rubber duck will drop from the ceiling when Digger uses his "points in the paint" line, and Digger will pull out a cap pistol and shoot the duck like Groucho Marx! He's definitely one of a kind. He brings fun to the telecast, intentionally or not.

Bob Knight: Perhaps the greatest coach in the history of the game. Extremely bright and knows the game inside out. I wish he would show more of his true personality in studio and while doing color. He will talk about blown calls by the refs, but I know he can bring more, like Al McGuire. Maybe he's a little uncomfortable with the role, but I'd love to see him let it all hang out as he did as a coach. He seems hesitant to question coaching strategies and really has not talked enough about officiating yet. Maybe he'll come out of his shell this season. I'd love to see him more in the studio with Gottlieb and Jay Williams. We might see the real Bob Knight and a few heated discussions.

Bill Raftery: I've already covered him with CBS, but I'll repeat that he is a real icon and a super human being. When he coached at Seton Hall, the officials voted him the toughest guy to work for, but everyone else loved him, including opposing coaches and every single member of the media. This ageless wonder has carved out a tremendous career for himself. I've known him for thirty-six years, and he hasn't changed one bit.

Jay Williams: Needs more experience but has potential. Still just a rookie but his on-air personality is very positive. Has good knowledge of the game because he played for one of the best coaches, Coach K. at Duke. But he still prepares very hard as he did as a player. He has excellent delivery.

Steve Bardo: Excellent, knows the game, very articulate. Somebody is holding him back.

Hubert Davis: Just like Bardo. Has the whole package. Should be doing more games.

Len Elmore: Should be doing more feature games. He's exceptional. He must have ticked somebody off.

Dan Dakich: Excellent knowledge and delivery. Future star.

Doris Burke: A real pro, works hard, and knows the game.

Sean Farnham: Tells it like it is. Knowledgeable, does his homework, and has a smooth delivery.

Myles Simon: Has all the intangibles but needs more airtime.

These talented people often become bigger than the sport that they cover with all of the power and influence that television generates today. Just like coaches, these people should be put under the microscope from time to time. Of course, these criticisms are just my humble opinion, and they should be taken with a grain of salt.

Fred Shabel, my college coach at Connecticut, used to say that it was not his job to evaluate our personal character, but he would be evaluating our skills every single day. Ditto to ESPN. Nothing personal here, fellas!

THE MEDIA

As a college basketball coach at Tufts University in a major sports town, Boston, I relished the opportunity to be interviewed by some of the legends of the media, such as Peter Gammons and Will McDonough, way back in the early 1970s when I was in my mid-twenties. It was basically Page 8 stuff in the Boston sports pages, but I respected those guys and felt honored to get me and my team even mentioned in their columns. Boston was a pro city and the *Boston Globe* and the *Boston Herald* would only write about us when we were on a roll. College hockey was bigger than college basketball in Boston. There were no beat writers covering us on a daily basis. We had to do something worthy of notice.

Years later, the *Boston Globe* treated me as one of its own when my 1988 Rhode Island Rams team made a run to the Sweet 16 in the NCAA Tournament, even featuring the Rams on the front page. It was a thrill to be recognized by a major writer in a major newspaper.

After my stint at Tufts, I moved to New York City in the spring of 1974 and remained in the Big Apple for twelve years where I coached at Columbia University and Fordham University. I was amazed at the coverage and attention we drew from so many newspapers there. When the Ivy League season began in January we would have game-day advance stories in the *New York Times*, *New York Post*, and *Daily News* every Friday when we played at home. At Fordham, pre-game and post-game coverage continued. Landing on the back page of the *New York Post* was really something. After a victory over one of our cross-town rivals, my wife and I would stay up for the early edition newspaper to arrive at a newsstand to relive the moment. A well-written game story was a treasure. We have scrapbooks filled with stories and columns by the great sportswriters of the day.

College basketball was a big media event in New York. The Knicks were the main event during fall and winter, but college basketball dwarfed college football in the Big Apple. Rutgers was undefeated until losing in the 1976 Final Four semifinals. Nearby Princeton won the 1975 National Invitation Tournament. St. John's fielded some pretty strong teams during that era, too.

New York had an abundance of exceptional sportswriters and television stars. Every Monday was media day at Mama Leone's, a famous Italian restaurant in the heart of the Theater District. All of the coaches and writers in the New York metropolitan area would convene to dine, socialize, and share stories in a casual setting. Every coach was given the opportunity to speak and to answer questions. Those luncheons were like *Saturday Night Live*. A coach either learned how to make people laugh or he was swallowed up by the competition. Jim Valvano (Iona), Bill Raftery (Seton Hall), and Lou Carnesecca (St. John's) were pretty challenging for P. J. Carlesimo (Wagner), Mike Krzyzewski (Army), and me. Nobody wanted to be called up before Raftery because his jokes would kill you.

On any given Monday, as many as twenty-five area sportswriters would gather at Mama Leone's with the New York City coaches. Great writers such as Gordon White of the *New York Times*, Steve

Serby of the *New York Post,* Mike Lupica of the *New York Daily News,* Jerry Izenberg of the *Newark Star-Ledger,* Bernie Beglane of *Long Island Press,* and Chuck Stogel of the *Gannett Westchester News* attended the luncheons. Sometimes visiting coaches, either in person or on phone hookups, would participate in the luncheon. Coaches from all over the country wanted to get coverage and boost their teams' rankings in the Top 25.

To get some ink in the Tuesday newspapers in New York, a coach had to be funny, entertaining, and controversial. All the coaches let their hair down and let it all hang out for the media. It was great stuff. Everybody loved being there. There was tremendous rapport and respect between the media and the coaches. If somebody was having a rough season, all the coaches would try to help the coach out. If a coach was getting a little cocky, the coaches would gang up on him until he got back in line. Because all the media and the coaches were making roughly the same money, there was little, if any, envy or jealousy. A coach or media person would need to check his ego along with his hat at Mama Leone's door.

Another favorite meeting ground for the media and coaches in the New York area was the original Runyon's at Fiftieth and Second avenues. It became a tradition for everybody to gather there after local college games to analyze and over analyze the night's games, stats, refs, bad calls, etc. Often sports trivia challenges ensued.

"It was a kind and gentler time and collegial," said Happy Fine, a New York–area writer who later worked for *Off the Glass Magazine* and SportsChannel, a forerunner of the current sports cable systems. "It was different from people trying to find something controversial to write about to advance their career. Coaches and players would come in and relationships would be built there at Runyon's."

Coaches hung out together although they competed hard on the floor and in recruiting. I don't know how it was in the rest of the country, but I thought New York was the best place for a coach to be from 1974 to 1986: lots of great sportswriters, lots of great coaches, and lots of interesting teams to cover. Coaches could lead normal lives. They did their interviews before and after the games. And they were allowed to occasionally speak candidly off the record. The Internet, whose bloggers hound coaches around the clock now, didn't exist.

Although writers might have been critical, they weren't mean spirited and ugly. They also gave coaches a chance to respond to their questions and didn't just spew a negative opinion without regard for facts or answers.

When I became the coach at Rhode Island, I missed the Mama Leone luncheons and the Runyon's gang, but I enjoyed a great relationship with Art Turgeon, the *Providence Journal* beat writer. Billy Reynolds, a former star basketball player at Brown, was a wonderful columnist and great storyteller for the same paper. I had close relationships with both of them and trusted both of them. They knew the game extremely well.

While I was coach of the Rams from 1986 to 1988, the state of Rhode Island went crazy over the basketball success of its major universities. Rick Pitino's Providence Friars went to the Final Four in 1987, and the next season my Rhode Island Rams made the Sweet 16. With no pro teams in the state, college basketball was really the only game in town for the media. College football at Rhode Island and Brown was only big in the tail-gaiting parking lots. While there was great competition between Rhode Island and Providence on the court, when one team got on a roll, and the other didn't, the state tended to get behind that winning team.

When I moved to Texas and into the Southwest Conference in 1988, there wasn't the camaraderie among the media that I was used to in the East. Football dominated the sports pages in Texas, where all of the SWC schools, except for Arkansas, were located. And in the 1980s, the Texas writers were covering NCAA probations more often than wins and losses.

All SWC member schools except for Arkansas and Rice were dealing with some sort of NCAA probation, which may have contributed to the negative atmosphere. The SWC members and writers seemed to have disdain for each other. Few outside of the Longhorn family liked Texas because of its power and influence. Since Texas basketball had been down, it didn't receive a lot of coverage, either.

I tried very hard to reach out to the entire state and get them interested in my basketball program. I went out and did interviews all over the place and tried to explain how my up-tempo style would work in the SWC. Beat writers from other schools were skeptical. I was hired by the University of Texas to bring my style of basketball down there and to create excitement at a school that had absolutely no fan base for hoops. I wanted the media to help spread the word and get fans excited about Texas basketball. Texas had only been to one NCAA Tournament (1979) in the fifteen years prior to my arrival in 1988.

During my ten years at UT, 90 percent of what *Austin American Statesman* columnist Kirk Bohls wrote about me was nice and flattering. A coach isn't going to get 100 percent support from the columnists anywhere, particularly in a town such as Austin with one major team to cover. The columnist has to appear objective. But I had fun with Kirk. There were some years when Kirk counted us out. At the end of the year when we went to the Elite Eight in 1990, I joked that he had pulled his groin jumping on the bandwagon.

I spent a total of sixteen years in the state of Texas, coaching at the University of Texas and later at the University of Houston. One of my all-time favorite writers was Randy Galloway—from the *Fort Worth Star-Telegram* and a radio personality in the Metroplex—

because he always did his homework and asked questions. Cathy Harasta and Kevin Blackistone, from the *Dallas Morning News*, gained my respect because they took the time to do interviews and asked great questions. Jonathan Feigen and Fran Blinebury, both from the *Houston Chronicle*; Al Carter, who worked for papers in Houston, San Antonio, and Dallas; and columnists Blackie Sherrod (*Dallas Morning News*) and Frank Luksa (*Dallas Morning News* and *Dallas Times Herald*) are also on my favorites list.

Gene Duffy is first class. My final beat writer at UH, Steve Campbell, covering the Cougars for the *Houston Chronicle*, is as fine a man as I have ever met. And, of course, my good longtime friend and co-author, Steve Richardson, is simply the best!

I have never turned down a media interview in my entire career. It puzzles me when a writer does a story on the coach and doesn't give the coach the benefit of an interview. Sometimes a coach deserves criticism from a columnist, but it's not right when a columnist fails to interview a coach and writes inaccurate things about him. Some sports editors will hold all their writers accountable, but sometimes it just boils down to selling newspapers, not credibility.

A negative story about me or my team served as motivational material. I called it bulletin board material and always cautioned my players not to speak words that might be used against us. I believed there was nothing like proving the media wrong. And when I proved the media wrong, I was not afraid to put it right back in their face.

It isn't fun in a profession where we all take ourselves too seriously. Reporters who don't do their homework, check the validity of their pronouncements, or just prefer to make stuff up deserve to be embarrassed. The majority of reporters are solid, hard-working, and talented people who take pride in their work. But there are a few who have no ethics and often seem to have an agenda. I feel sorry for them. They just appear to be miserable people. They have no compassion for coaches or players. Perhaps chalk it up to jealousy.

I believe coaches should give writers, especially their beat writer, as much access as possible. Some coaches close their practices possibly because they believe a reporter will expose the game plan. For the most part, the beat writers, often traveling with the team and sharing a road-game meal, truly get to know the players and the coaches this way. They develop trust. I have had open practice and film sessions with reporters my entire career. It gives them an idea of what we are doing and why we are planning to follow a certain game plan. It makes their job easier too.

To this day, I am baffled by a particular writer's complete avoidance of me, preferring to write negative opinion pieces without ever calling or asking for an interview. I don't remember ever seeing him at a game, but on several occasions I opened my home-delivered *Houston Chronicle* and read a nasty column by this writer, Richard Justice. Or, sometimes a friend would forward me one of his negative blogs. The frequency of these blogs seemed to accelerate during the 2008–09 season to the point where they were becoming laughable.

My wife would ask me about this guy and what I had done to him. He never bothered to call and at least get my side of a story to make it fair and balanced, like one would expect from a professional journalist. Then one day we got our chance to confront this writer in person.

Susie and I were returning from the 2009 Final Four in Detroit when Susie noticed Justice onboard our aircraft. Susie recognized him first from his photo with his column. He sat several rows in front of us. Susie contemplated walking up the aisle to meet him but decided to wait. Because he apparently boarded without any luggage she presumed that he would have to wait with the rest of us to retrieve his baggage. She said she just wanted to introduce herself and open the door to communication. She has always enjoyed the camaraderie that we have had with writers. Susie described her odd encounter with Richard Justice as follows:

"I raced off the plane to make sure that I made it to the baggage claim area before all the bags arrived. I lost sight of columnist Richard Justice, who deplaned ahead of us. When I arrived at our assigned carousel, I did not see him. I thought I had missed my opportunity before I saw a bag drop with his ID attached.

"Pretty soon everyone except for Mr. Justice had retrieved their bags. The lone bag circled several times until the carousel finally stopped. An airline baggage attendant asked us if we knew the owner of the lone bag. We replied that we did, and we were waiting for him to retrieve it. Now, we felt obligated to guard his bag. Forty-five minutes had passed. I scoured the airport landscape once again in hopes of spotting him. Across the numerous baggage carousels in a corner in an unlit area I finally saw him. Suddenly, he disappeared behind a post. Then, his head popped out from behind the post and disappeared again like in a child's game of hide and seek. It was obvious to me that he was hiding from us. I decided I would end the silliness by just walking over to him and introducing myself.

"Justice seemed very uncomfortable when I tapped him on the shoulder and forced him to acknowledge me. He did shake my extended hand. And I said that Tom was waiting by his bag and that he should come over and say hello. After a moment he joined us at the baggage carousel where we had a brief and friendly exchange. Tom politely extended his hand and made a light comment about how difficult the life of a columnist must be."

For the most part, the writers I met in my thirty-six years of head coaching have been fun, interesting, and gregarious people. I never had much of a problem with anyone else in Texas. Getting to know the media is important. Developing relationships is more important. I feel over the years I have developed a lot of good relationships with the media. I consider most of them lifetime friends. One of our very best friends in life is Happy Fine, a wonderful, colorful character who could be counted among the top journalists in the country, if things had gone his way in that field. He has become a highly successful manager with Connors Sports Flooring.

All in all, I think dealing with media has been a lot of fun. I hope most of them feel the same way.

AFTERWORD

COACHING
THEN AND NOW,
1971-2010

oaching at the collegiate level has never been easy, but the challenges in the twenty-first century are far more complex and competitive than ever before. Basketball is definitely a business where many of the top schools pay their men's basketball coaches large salaries and, in turn, expect to make large revenues from home attendance, television appearances, and NCAA Tournament berths.

The top coaches of today—Duke's Mike Krzyzewski, Michigan State's Tom Izzo, Kansas' Bill Self, and Connecticut's Jim Calhoun, for example—make in the single-digit millions each year with their compensation packages that include base salaries, shoe contracts, camps, and other perks and incentives. Back in the 1970s and 1980s, college basketball had yet to produce large revenues. In turn, coaches still had salaries in line with tenured professors.

UCLA's highly successful coach John Wooden retired in 1975 with a salary of $42,000, while I was making $35,000 at Columbia University. Eleven years later, Houston's Guy V. Lewis retired in 1986 after making five Final Fours during his career, but he was making only a few thousand more than I was earning at Fordham

University at the same time.

In that era, lawyers and agents were not big players in the game of college basketball. Now, they are all over the place as well as some shadowy AAU summer coaches and supporters. They, not the high school coaches, control the recruiting.

Today, the NCAA enforcement staff is at least platoon sized, but back in the 1960s and into the 1970s there might have been one or two investigators and a much thinner rulebook. A lot of people think that many schools were cheating back in the 1960s and 1970s, which may be the truth, but it was an entirely different rulebook and alumni and boosters were allowed to recruit.

Nobody expected the NCAA to expose much because they were a two-man gang with a peashooter, but they were catching some of the bad boys nonetheless.

Coach Tates Locke was found guilty of forty violations while trying to build Clemson into a power program in the mid-1970s.

Southwestern Louisiana's basketball program received a two-year death penalty for NCAA violations in 1973–75.

In the early 1970s, the NCAA even hung a six-year probation on tiny Centenary College of Louisiana basically for daring to play star freshman center Robert Parrish following a dispute over a conversion of his entrance grade-point average.

The biggest fish was never caught during that earlier era. After John Wooden retired there were an awful lot of rumors about power broker and UCLA booster Sam Gilbert and his involvement with recruiting for the Bruins. I suspect that Coach Wooden didn't want to know, and his athletic director, J. D. Morgan, had to be the most naïve person in the world after reading some of the stories about Sam Gilbert.

There was a recent HBO special on the magical Bruin run starting in 1964 through Wooden's last season in 1975. Gilbert seemed to appear prominently on the UCLA scene after the 1967–68 season when UCLA athletic department officials asked Gilbert to step in and keep star players Lucius Allen and Lew Alcindor from transferring out of UCLA. After helping Alcindor and Allen stay in Westwood, apparently Gilbert became actively involved in all facets of UCLA basketball.

In December of 1981, UCLA was found guilty of nine violations, which forced the Bruins to vacate their second-place finish in the 1980 NCAA Tournament. They were placed on two years probation and banned from the 1982 NCAA Tournament. Sam Gilbert was also banished from the UCLA program after it was disclosed that he signed a promissory note so that a Bruin player could buy a car. Larry Farmer was the coach who suffered the most from the scandal.

It is hard to believe today that Gilbert's involvement at UCLA would have gone under the radar as long as it apparently did for a team that won a record ten NCAA championships from 1964 to 1975. With the help of the Internet (ESPN.com, Yahoo!, Google, Facebook, and Twitter) and twenty-four seven sports on radio and television, there are few secrets left in college basketball. The NCAA can't always prove something is going on, but the enforcement staff is at least sniffing around the edges. They now get plenty of assistance from the Internet media.

When I left Houston in the spring of 2010, it seemed as if the whole coaching world was exploding all over the country. High-profile coaches were getting arrested for DUIs, narcotics, and shoplifting, either before or after they were fired. It seems like more schools are under investigation than ever.

One of the splashiest stories was the saga of Louisville coach Rick Pitino who had to endure a well-publicized trial of the wife of a former Louisville basketball equipment manager. In 2003, Pitino had a sexual encounter with the woman, Karen Sypher, who was on trial during the summer of 2010. In a sensational trial, she was found guilty of trying to extort him for money and gifts after the encounter.

Elsewhere, we've seen fraud in ACT and SAT testing and phony prep schools helping to prostitute the recruiting process. "Pinch-hitting"—an imposter actually takes the prospect's ACT or SAT test—sometimes occurs. And I routinely and skeptically have watched prospects increase their entrance test scores and grades overnight. A senior prospect has a 1.8 grade-point average, then gets a 4.0 grade-point at his new prep school, passes all his core requirements, and comes up with a 1050 SAT score. All of a sudden, he is eligible to play at a Division I school. Two years later the player leaves for the NBA, somebody blows the whistle, the school vacates the wins, the coach moves on to another school, and his record never reflects the forfeits.

See John Calipari, who perfected the dance from Memphis to Kentucky around a test-score scandal involving standout guard Derrick Rose, now a Chicago Bull. Coach Cal perhaps had nothing to do with the player's amazing improvement. But his overall coaching record should reflect the vacated NCAA Tournament wins, the entire season at Memphis in 2007–08, and his 1995–96 season at UMASS, which was also vacated. Sorry Coach Cal, but those wins should be removed from a coach's personal win/loss record, otherwise what is the penalty for using ineligible players?

In a March 10, 2010, *Wall Street Journal* article, former Michigan president James Duderstadt said, "College hoops was the cesspool of college sports." Since then ESPN's Dana O'Neil and Gene Wojciechowski have written scathing articles. O'Neil wrote an article on July 22, 2010, titled, "What's Wrong with College Basketball," which every college president and athletic director must read. She polled twenty of the highest-profile coaches in the country, and the results were shocking. All of the coaches were from the top six conferences in the country. Eight out of the twenty coaches interviewed said, "No, they didn't trust their peers." Five of these coaches said they "trusted only 10 of their peers." Although these quoted coaches were promised anonymity, it doesn't reflect favorably on the coaching profession.

And in *USA Today*, Big Ten commissioner Jim Delany was quoted as saying on August 16, 2010: "There is a loss of confidence among many college coaches that the rules are being complied with. The best way I can describe it is a sense of cynicism. I am talking about the youth programs (AAU), the money that's being used to influence recruiting. And ultimately the buying of players, either through third parties or though coaches and third parties-agents. Make no mistake it is happening, it's a corruption issue." I have never seen a conference commissioner make such accusatory remarks.

I devoted an entire chapter to the problems with AAU and summer basketball and the characters that run it. In the summer of 2010, the NCAA put Arizona on probation and claimed that its former head coach, Lute Olson, violated major rules regarding the sponsorship of an AAU tournament and at least one AAU program where future Arizona recruits were playing. According to an article by ESPN.com's Andy Katz, Olson, a Naismith Basketball Hall of Fame coach, was named as the person responsible for urging Wildcat boosters to step up and financially support an AAU event that was held on Arizona's campus. The boosters came through to the tune of almost $200,000. Olson admitted that he broke some rules but recanted after Arizona was hit with probation.

The NCAA report claims that Olson violated major rules and that "he did not foster a climate of compliance within his staff." The NCAA gave the seventy-five-year-old Olson, who admitted the violations, a "pass" because of his age, his poor health because of stroke, and the fact he probably wouldn't return to coaching. I can't see why any coach like Lute Olson would risk it all just to get recruits. You don't have to cheat to win at Arizona. But maybe the pressure to win is getting to a lot of coaches.

The program of another Naismith Basketball Hall of Fame coach—Jim Calhoun—has recently been under an NCAA investigation. UConn has admitted to major NCAA rules violations for improper telephone calls and texts and illegal benefits to recruits and giving tickets to high school coaches and others. The Huskies have self-imposed some penalties already. While Calhoun has been cited by the NCAA for failing to promote an atmosphere of compliance, UConn is fighting that charge. Calhoun has had a spotless record in the past, and I personally don't think Calhoun should be responsible for the phone calls or texts of assistants. The UConn compliance office should be monitoring those. Coaches cannot find the time to check all of the assistant coaches' telephone calls.

Some college presidents and athletic directors have to accept some of the blame because they created the starting point of this vicious cycle. They negotiate the ridiculously lucrative contracts for coaches, who usually accept the money and the pressure to win big, or move on to another school. And then sadly some of these coaches accept shortcuts to keep winning. It's absolutely insane for a coach to risk millions of dollars by intentionally breaking NCAA rules, but it is happening all over the place.

When I was being courted by Rutgers and Texas in the spring of 1988, things were changing. I was shocked to see what they were offering compared to what I was making at Rhode Island. Money is the root of all evil, and it was clear that schools were entering an evil world. By taking the Texas job, I made many times over what I was being paid at Rhode Island. Shoe contracts were also going through the ceiling. I went from making $25,000 with Reebok to $85,000 at

Texas within twelve months. It was mind blowing to me. And that's nothing compared to what it is today.

Of course the pressure increased exponentially with the big paychecks. If a coach's lucrative salary was published, the fans and the administration usually expected good results. And once a coach was making big money, he didn't want to fail and lose the big bucks that were flowing into his bank account. Looking back, it was pure insanity on the part of colleges and the administrators who set up the system and were calling the shots.

Now it's highly unusual to find a big-time school where a chancellor or an athletic director makes even one-half of what a basketball or football coach makes. It's absolutely upside down. Presidents last an average of four years at a school. Athletic directors are now moving on at the same pace as coaches. So people who hire coaches often move on themselves while the coach is still there. And faculty members, whose salaries often are frozen year after year because of university budget cuts, then read that the football or basketball coach just got an extension and a $500,000 raise. They think, "Wait a minute, we are tenured professors. We are teaching the students, and we are making $60,000 and this guy is making $600,000 base pay? It makes no sense."

The three biggest scandals on the burner before this book reached the printing stage were more than minor events. The biggest story involved Auburn's star quarterback Cam Newton. After months of rumors and reports, it was ruled that Cam Newton was eligible even though his father was openly shopping Cam to Mississippi State while Cam was attending Blinn Junior College in Brenham, Texas. The NCAA ruled that Cam knew nothing about his father's transgressions despite the fact that Cam and his father openly spoke about how close they actually were. Cam stated that he never made any decisions in his life without consulting his father, Cecil. The NCAA has either changed its rules or they now also believe in Santa Claus and the Easter Bunny! It's totally fine now for recruiters to pay off parents, relatives, or friends of a recruit as long as the athlete doesn't know what's going on. Wow, the NCAA has just opened a can of maggots that they may never recover from. There isn't a coach in any sport in the NCAA that can believe how the NCAA ruled in Cam Newton's case.

Another interesting ruling was handed down that allowed multiple Ohio State football players to play in this year's Sugar Bowl despite committing numerous major violations. These players sold their jerseys, rings, and Ohio State gifts to the owner of a tattoo parlor and most made thousands of dollars in the process. The NCAA ruled that the guilty players could play in the bowl game but they had to sit out the first five games in 2011! Every skeptic believes the Buckeye players were allowed to play so that the Sugar Bowl would still be sold out and that the television ratings would not be affected. I have a hard time arguing with these skeptics. Coach Jim Tressell must also believe in the Easter Bunny because he stated that all of the guilty players have promised to return for another season at Ohio State to serve out their suspensions. Yeah, right!

Last and certainly not least is the saga of Bruce Pearl, the head basketball coach at Tennessee. Bruce admitted that he lied to NCAA investigators during an interview regarding some unofficial visits to his house party before the prospects were seniors. Bruce told the NCAA investigators, who had pictures from the party, that it never happened and that he didn't recognize the house in the pictures. A few weeks later Pearl recanted and said he lied and that he was guilty of lying to the NCAA. SEC commissioner Mike Slive suspended Bruce Pearl from coaching eight games of the 2010–11 season. Apparently Pearl was also fined a significant amount by the president at Tennessee. People like ESPN's Jay Bilas have been publicly critical of Tennessee's decision to retain Pearl as their coach or for not giving him a harsher penalty. Pearl is not the only coach that has been caught lying to the NCAA, and I don't think he should be fired. A one-year suspension and forfeit of his paycheck to The Jimmy V. Foundation would be a sufficient penalty and also serve a great cause. Why should Tennessee be able to keep his money? They hired him. By sitting out a year and losing a year's pay he would learn a great lesson and so would the University of Tennessee. The NCAA would also gain some badly needed respect from the general public by helping to find a cure for cancer.

The pressure to win, the cutting of corners by some coaches, and the grab for the cash have created a sometimes shadowy side of college coaching that I won't miss.

I pride myself on never breaking any NCAA rules during my thirty-six years as a college head coach. During my six years at Houston, I was approached by more than one shaky character who asked for a job on my staff or plain hard cash to deliver a player. Once a coach gets in bed with those people, they own him forever. The coach is a phone call or an audiotape away from being fired and shamed forever. It just takes one DUI in today's unforgiving world, and a coach's career can be over. Cutting a deal with an agent or an AAU coach can only lead to future shame and embarrassment.

I don't feel sorry for any coach who intentionally breaks rules to gain an advantage. Do it the right way, trust your ability to coach, and you will live to face your children and grandchildren. Be a solid example for your university or college, players, and your family.

I have been able to walk away after 648 wins with all of my dignity intact. I'm lucky. But I always tried to do things within the rules and for the right reasons. To do that at seven schools during four different decades has been gratifying. It has been a wild, fun ride full of experiences I will never forget.

INDEX

251

Since starting at Tufts in 1971–72, **Tom Penders** has excelled as a college coach at seven schools, six on the Division I level. No other major college coach has coached at more schools, and only four others have equaled his seven college coaching stops. In compiling 648 victories during a 36-year college career, Penders coached 1,086 games and led teams to 11 NCAA Tournaments, eight National Invitation Tournaments, and two College Basketball Invitationals.

Penders, who played basketball and baseball at the University of Connecticut from 1964 to 1967, is also one of eight coaches to have taken four different schools (Rhode Island, Texas, George Washington, and Houston) to the Division I NCAA Tournament. At his latest stop, Houston, Penders engineered the Cougars' first NCAA Tournament trip in eighteen years. He is the only coach in Houston history to win eighteen games or more six straight seasons.

Steve Richardson, a Dallas-based freelance writer, has covered college and pro sports since the late 1970s. He worked at the *Kansas City Star* and later at the *Dallas Morning News* for more than twenty years combined. He has written, collaborated, or edited twelve previous books. His latest release was in the fall of 2010, *The Cotton Bowl Classic Football Vault: The History of a Proud Texas Tradition.*

His other titles are *University of Texas Football Vault: A Story of the Texas Longhorns; A Century of Sports: The Centennial Book of the Missouri Valley Conference; Ricky Williams: Dreadlocks to Ditka; Kelvin Sampson: The OU Basketball Story;* and *Tales from the Texas Longhorns.* Richardson has had three books released by Triumph Books: *Then Osborne Said to Rozier, Then Pinkel Said to Smith,* and *100 Things Oklahoma Fans Should Know and Do Before They Die.*